OPEN BORDERS, NONALIGNMENT, AND THE POLITICAL EVOLUTION OF YUGOSLAVIA

OPEN BORDERS,
NONALIGNMENT, AND THE
POLITICAL EVOLUTION
OF YUGOSLAVIA

———◆◆◆———

William Zimmerman

PRINCETON UNIVERSITY PRESS, PRINCETON, NEW JERSEY

Copyright © 1987 by Princeton University Press
Published by Princeton University Press, 41 William Street,
Princeton, New Jersey 08540
In the United Kingdom: Princeton University Press,
Guildford, Surrey

Parts of chapter 4 are taken from *Political Development in
Eastern Europe*, edited by Jan Triska and Paul M. Cocks.
Copyright © 1977 Praeger Publishers, Inc. Reprinted by
permission of Praeger Publishers.

All Rights Reserved

Library of Congress Cataloging in Publication Data will
be found on the last printed page of this book

ISBN 0-691-07730-4

Publication of this book has been aided by a grant
from the Whitney Darrow Fund of Princeton University Press

This book has been composed in Linotron Times Roman

Clothbound editions of Princeton University Press books
are printed on acid-free paper, and binding materials
are chosen for strength and durability. Paperbacks, although
satisfactory for personal collections, are not usually
suitable for library rebinding

Printed in the United States of America by Princeton
University Press, Princeton, New Jersey

CONTENTS

TABLES

ACKNOWLEDGMENTS

It has long been my intention to write a book about Yugoslavia, a country that has fascinated me for years. While the views expressed herein are entirely my own, one nice result of having finished such a book is the opportunity it provides to acknowledge my indebtedness to those who over the years have shared their knowledge of Yugoslavia with me or who have otherwise facilitated my research efforts. The list of Yugoslavs who have befriended me is a very long one indeed, and my interviews, conversations, and arguments with them have been an essential backdrop to this book. It has benefited particularly from the comments and expertise of Ivo Baucic and Dusan Bilandzic. Among Western scholars, I am particularly indebted to the comments on early versions of this manuscript by Steven Burg, Paul Costolanski, A. Ross Johnson, Paul Shoup, and Alvin Rubinstein. Jan Triska first encouraged me to think of how the Yugoslav regime governed the workers abroad.

A Fulbright-Hays grant made possible my longest stay in Yugoslavia, and the hospitality of the Institute for International Politics and Trade (Belgrade) made that stay a memorable and enjoyable experience. I was able to pursue my interest in the Yugoslav workers' migration through a grant by the Ford Foundation, which in turn permitted a research stay at Stanford University. The actual writing of the bulk of the book was made possible by a contract from the United States Department of State. The University of Michigan and especially its Center for Russian and East European Studies and its Institute for Public Policy Studies have consistently provided me with an environment conducive to scholarly endeavors. I owe special thanks to Dean Peter Steiner whose endearing words, "Get away from here and finish that book," supported my efforts to combine administration and research. Marysia Ostafin, Judy Jackson, and Jacquin Brendle typed various incarnations of this manuscript with competence and tolerance.

Some of those partial incarnations were in other places. My thanks are to the journals, *Studies in Comparative Communism* and *Problems of Communism*, and to Macmillan, St. Martin's Press, and Praeger for permission to incorporate expansions of previous work into this volume, as well as to the editors, Paul Cocks and Jan Triska and Michael Sodaro and Sharon L. Wolchik, of volumes in which earlier versions of parts of this study previously appeared.

The book is dedicated to Alice, Carl, and Fred, who have been an unmitigated joy to their father.

OPEN BORDERS, NONALIGNMENT,
AND THE POLITICAL EVOLUTION
OF YUGOSLAVIA

1

INTRODUCTION

In the mid-1980s, the era in which the World War II Partisan generation ruled the Socialist Federal Republic of Yugoslavia was coming rapidly to an end. (Yugoslavia consists of six republics, Bosnia-Hercegovina, Croatia, Macedonia, Montenegro, Slovenia, and Serbia; and, within the Republic of Serbia, two autonomous provinces, Vojvodina and Kosovo.) Not only did Josip Broz (Tito) finally die (in 1980) after some thirty-five years as the "first real Yugoslav national leader" [Shoup, 1968], but so too did Edvard Kardelj and Vladimir Bakaric, the two other most prominent Partisan leaders who remained part of the central political leadership throughout the course of the post-World War II period. Other members of the elderly Yugoslav political elite are almost certain to pass from the political scene in the near future, and Yugoslavia will be governed in the relatively near future by a new political generation made up, not of Partisans, much less *prvoborci* (the first fighters in World War II), but rather of persons raised and socialized almost entirely in the Tito era.

Whatever else that older generation and Tito in particular accomplished over thirty-five years, they and "New" Yugoslavia survived. For any modern state that is no mean feat. As philatelists have long known, and students of comparative politics have more recently discovered, states come and go with some regularity. T. Robert Gurr [1974] has shown that the average duration of a polity in the nineteenth and twentieth centuries has been thirty-two years.

Yugoslavia's continuing political independence is all the more impressive when one contemplates the challenges that Yugoslavia, in particular, has faced. The Yugoslavs have withstood vigorous efforts by Stalin to bring down the Tito regime—and in the process to impose satellite status on Yugoslavia. Under Tito's leadership, Yugoslavia managed (through varying admixtures of accommodation and repression) to maintain some degree of national cohesion despite the forces, external and internal, which have rendered this task difficult. For example, Yugoslavia is one of the few countries in the contemporary world about which it may be properly said that there exist persons outside the country who are actively dedicated to tearing it asunder by violent means. The most obvious are the Croatian nationalist groups, many of them related in some way to the pre-1945 *Ustasa*, a separatist-terrorist movement that ruled Croatia under German aegis during World War II. Yugoslavia is also a state whose territorial integrity has been

3

challenged throughout the postwar period. Not until 1975, when the boundaries between Italy and Yugoslavia became permanently fixed, were formal disputes with foreign states over the extent of Yugoslav domains resolved. Even in the mid-1980s Bulgaria seems to the Yugoslavs to behave as though it has not abandoned its desire to reclaim territories now incorporated into Yugoslavia as the Republic of Macedonia.

Furthermore, Yugoslavia has seemed an exception—it turns out there are many—to the old generalization that modernization increases symbolic attachment to the nation state at the expense of both more universal and more parochial institutions. As John de Lamater has demonstrated [1969], increasing development has produced in Yugoslavia, both within and between republics, increasing symbolic attachment to the republic rather than to the Federation. This situation has been exacerbated by the enormous and continuing economic gap between the wealthiest and poorest republics and autonomous provinces. As we shall see, the gross social product per capita of the Republic of Slovenia, for example, roughly approximates that of central Italy, while the gross social product per capita of the autonomous province of Kosovo is comparable to that of Congo (Brazzaville), Ghana, or Liberia.

The survival of independent Yugoslavia is equally remarkable when one considers the divergent attitudes about Yugoslav independence to be found among Yugoslav elites and potential counterelites. Without putting too fine a point on the matter, it can be said that by no means all Yugoslavs have agreed with Leo Mates, former Yugoslav Ambassador to the United States, "that the desire to preserve independence is the prime consideration in formulating foreign policy" [1972, p. 111]. For a sizable number of Yugoslav citizens, a major consideration has been not preserving the independence and sovereignty of Yugoslavia, but rather securing independence of a component part of the country *from* Yugoslavia.

The 1981 riots in Kosovo, which is heavily Albanian ethnically, are only the most recent manifestation of that proclivity. In the late 1960s, some influential Slovenes voiced feelings that the Republic of Slovenia would be better off outside Yugoslavia. A nationalist upsurge in Croatia in 1971, culminating in a strike at Zagreb University, likewise provided the occasion for dramatic calls for republican autonomy, the effects of which would have been the virtual dismantling of the Yugoslav Federation.

In the mid-1980s, moreover, Yugoslavia faces many of the same issues it confronted throughout the Tito era and some additional ones as well. As any reader of the *New York Times* is aware, Yugoslavia has an external debt in excess of $20,000,000,000; enormous unemployment; shortages in electricity, detergents, coffee, cooking oil, and raw materials; and double-digit inflation. All these problems, coupled with the departure of the Partisan generation from the Yugoslav political stage, make this an especially apt occasion for a kind of stock-taking of important trends in Yugoslav political development, for an effort to sort out the elements of continuity and change in the evolution of Yugoslav elite strategies for maintaining independence and reinforcing legitimacy, and to attempt to discover how these in turn influence the evolution of Yugoslav political institutions, processes, and major policy orientations.

That is the task of this monograph, which I hope will be of interest both to policymakers and to analysts of communist systems. On its intrinsic merits, it should be.

For the policymaker, Yugoslavia has been and very likely will continue to be of interest politically. Certainly, Yugoslavia has been politically significant as an example in the past. Alvin Rubinstein [1970] found the Yugoslav pattern influential in Nasser's Egypt. Central Yugoslav themes have found responsive chords in Eastern Europe as well. There was a direct link between the Soviet-Yugoslav *rapprochement* in 1955—which seemed to portend the legitimacy of national communism in Eastern Europe—and the 1956 Hungarian and Polish events. Many of the features of Yugoslav communism that have lent credence to Yugoslav claims of distinctiveness have at various times found an echo among change-oriented elites in Eastern Europe: workers' self-management, market socialism, Yugoslavia's concomitant commitment to economic links with the global economy. The Hungarian New Economic Mechanism has clear intellectual roots in Yugoslav market socialism as do the aspirations of moderate Polish reformers to institutionalize authentic workers' self-management as a vehicle for closing the gap between the Polish regime and society.

The extent to which Yugoslavia, a country beset with precisely the ills—unemployment, high inflation—that would acutely distress East Europeans socialized in a world of underemployment and putatively inflation-free planned prices, will continue to be of direct political relevance is an area about which persons may reasonably disagree [Korbonski in Vucinich, ed., 1982]. Policymakers should, however, realize that Yugoslavia will continue to be of relevance, indirectly, to those East European elites who couple in their minds the notions of independence and domestic political experimentation.

Likewise, Yugoslavia would still be of interest to policymakers for its international political role even if one accepted the false premise that politically Yugoslavia is indistinguishable from Soviet-type communist systems; or, which is a possibility, if the Yugoslav political system were to become much closer than it is currently to its Soviet counterpart. There are alternative Yugoslavias which one can imagine that would be far less disposed to challenge the Soviet Union's direct or indirect efforts to harness the nonaligned movement to its interests, just as there are Yugoslavias one can envisage that would be more pro-Western and more oriented toward Europe.

Nevertheless, for the policymaker, the central significance of Yugoslavia is strategic. It is difficult to imagine any likely scenarios in which that importance would diminish over the intermediate haul. While strategically Yugoslavia does not constitute a threat to the Soviet Union, it does represent a considerable opportunity for Soviet global force projection. The Slovenian Alps are an obvious natural obstacle to any Soviet incursion into Italy. Yugoslav airspace facilitates direct Soviet aid to states in the Middle East. Increased access to Yugoslav ports would greatly enhance Soviet naval power projection in the Mediterranean—especially since the U.S.S.R. is to some degree constrained by the terms of the Montreux Convention relating to access between the Black Sea and the Mediterranean through the Dardanelles [Ra'anan, 1977]. Finally, Yugoslavia serves as a buffer between the Warsaw Treaty Organization states and Albania. For the policymaker, Yugoslavia's strategic significance almost renders irrelevant the issue of its continuing political significance, either as exemplar for Eastern Europe or as a force among small, primarily nonaligned states of the world.

To the scholar in the academy, by contrast, the remarkable pattern of Yugoslavia's political evolution remains the major reason why Yugoslavia continues to entrance. The study of communist systems is, in the technical sense that Thomas S. Kuhn [1962] uses to depict an unstable science, in a crisis. The common assumptions required of a normal science are no longer tenable as a starting point for the analysis of the entire class of communist systems, while the dimensions of a new paradigm are not yet clear. Much of the reason why this is so pertains to Yugoslavia and the ways Yugoslav reality has often failed to mesh with our assumptions about communist political systems.

Those assumptions have been governed, in turn, by our images of the Soviet Union and of the Soviet Union's relationship with its East European allies. Out of our attention to assessments of the nature of the Soviet political system and of the distinguishing characteristics of Soviet-East European relations emerged the two closely related paradigms that defined the general consensus of communist studies for the better part of the 1950s and 1960s: the Soviet and satellite ''models.''

The Soviet and satellite models depicted systems with similar patterns of regime-societal relations, intra-elite attributes, and public policy features. Each model described a political system characterized by low trust in the citizenry on the part of the leaders in the respective states. In such states, the sorts and sources of influence to which the citizenry were exposed were controlled through the regime's virtual monopoly over the socialization process and the political system's extensive penetration of the society. In neither case was there a substantial role for autonomous actors within the system. In both images, similarly, the regime was insulated from society; the behaviorally relevant inputs originated in the political system itself and not in society. The highly politicized society was juxtaposed to intra-elite relations where the high unity of command connoted a polity almost devoid of high politics, except when succession was at issue. Finally, there were several public policy features that were an integral, though not often articulated, dimension of both models: planners', rather than consumers', sovereignty prevailed. Nationalization was widespread. Capitalism, the capital market, and capitalists—foreign and domestic—were eliminated. Comparatively egalitarian wage policies were introduced and full employment approximated through the guise, primarily, of "political" factories and massive underemployment.

The Soviet and satellite models diverged in the assumptions each made about the relationship of the state and society to the international environment. While the image of the Soviet-style system shared little in common with traditional approaches to comparative politics, it did presume, as did such major overall approaches as David Easton's [1953] and Gabriel Almond's [1960], that sources external to the nation state were not of major consequence in explaining the state's political development. Rather, in its relationship to the international environment, the Soviet-type system was thought of as an essentially closed system. In that respect, the Soviet model was similar to the billiard-ball model of the traditional states-as-actors approach to international politics. Great attention was attached to ensuring the impermeability of the nation state's boundaries, and nonnational actors played no part in the internal policy process. Ideas and influences originating from outside the system were systematically prevented from entering the country, and the outflow of the state's citizenry was rigidly regulated. Consistent further with the closed system imagery, Soviet-type political systems were economically autarkic.

In the satellite imagery, by contrast, the nation state is highly penetrated and national-international linkage is the key to explaining internal political development. The penetration, however, originates from only a single source; other sources of influence, even those emanating from other satellites, are excluded. Each satellite was connected, in Karl Deutsch's terms [in Farrell, ed., 1966, p. 7], to a "decision center outside the state, from which decisions inside the state . . . [can] be predicted." Taken to its logical conclusion, the satellite imagery is one in which the putative nation state is merely yet another instance of a traditional political institution having been transformed by Moscow into a transmission belt, i.e., a mechanism for the downward communication of commands. And, indeed, in the most cohesive years of the Soviet bloc, Bulgaria actually voted against the Soviet

Union fewer times in the United Nations General Assembly than did the Ukrainian SSR [Hovet, 1960]. In short, there really was a time when Zbigniew Brzezinski and Mikhail Suslov had little quarrel in describing the distinguishing features of communist systems and when the boundaries that set off Soviet-type systems from other political systems were pronounced.

Events, however, have a way of outpacing models. In the 1950s, who was a communist, or what was a communist system was scarcely at issue. By the end of the 1960s, no single statement pertaining to the nature of the party or the relationship of the party to society or the political system could embrace the highly dissimilar variations among those professing to be communists. In the 1950s, it had been plausible to extrapolate from Soviet-East European relations to an overall depiction of relations among communist states—even though the 1948 Soviet-Yugoslav conflict provided an early indication of the limits of such an approach. By the end of the 1960s, the Sino-Soviet split and the independent positions of Albania, Cuba, North Korea, and North Vietnam precluded such a possibility.

With regard to Eastern Europe, similarly, the satellite and Soviet paradigms also failed to provide a highly accurate fit with the reality of the majority of communist states. At a minimum, "domesticism" (in Brzezinski's term)—with its implication that the focus of the decisional center is within the state—characterized the erstwhile satellites. Romania, the state in Eastern Europe that most approximated the traditional Soviet model internally, became the one whose relations with the U.S.S.R. were most at variance with traditional notions of Soviet-East European relations. By the onset of the 1970s, all the states of Eastern Europe had lost the isolation from the noncommunist world that typified the 1950s. They had in many instances substantially increased their ties with external sources other than the U.S.S.R. and reduced correspondingly the extent of penetration by the Soviet Union. Equally important, in some East European systems the societies have been depoliticized to an appreciable degree; the demand for affirmation has been replaced by regime tolerance of mere compliance on the part of the citizenry: in Hungary, most notably, Stalin's "He who is not with us, is against us" has been replaced by Janos Kadar's "He who is not against us, is with us."

Even with respect to the Soviet Union there has been much intellectual ferment and recognition of ways in which the Soviet Union diverges from the traditional "Soviet" model. Whether today the majority of Western specialists would employ the traditional paradigm is a moot point at best. The disfavor into which concepts such as totalitarianism and its intellectual offshoots, "mature totalitarianism," the "administered society" et al., have fallen in recent years suggests otherwise. There has been widespread recognition of the persisting impact of traditional Russian political culture on the Soviet polity, of the increased social differentiation and articulation of a growingly complex industrial society, and of the ubiquity of high politics.

It has been Yugoslav reality, however, that has been at cross purposes for the longest duration with expectations framed by the Soviet and satellite models. For one thing, Yugoslav-Soviet relations early on (by 1948 at the latest) revealed that there were fundamentally divergent behavioral consequences for communist states implied by the two models and that this constituted an intrinsic flaw in Stalinism as a form of interstate relations. In 1948, Stalin broke with Tito—not the reverse, as is often implied. That break demonstrated that a Soviet-type system could resist efforts, by means short of war, at penetration and domination by a great power, including the Soviet Union. In this respect, Yugoslavia's experience was but the first chapter in a book, the recurring plot of which centers on Soviet efforts to induce behavior on the part of a Soviet-type state typical of that of a satellite. In this story the end of each chapter is similar: the Soviet effort fails each time because states that approximate the Soviet model are organized so as to make them distinctively able to resist the pressures of imperial states, even when the state is the Motherland of Socialism herself. More importantly, after Stalin's abortive effort to transform Yugoslavia into a Soviet satellite, Yugoslavia evolved in ways that were strikingly anomalous when framed against expectations based on either the Soviet or satellite models.

To give but a couple of striking examples. For fifteen years after World War II, the prevailing attitude in Yugoslavia toward working abroad meshed with that which traditionally prevailed in other communist systems: to go abroad amounted to treason and political emigration. From 1960 on, however, Yugoslav workers went abroad, to capitalist Western Europe mainly, in such profusion (even during the stagflationary decade, 1973-1982) that one could speak of them as a seventh republic. (See below, Chapters 4 and 5.)

In like fashion one could easily assess Yugoslav federalism in 1946 from the perspective of the Soviet model. The constitution adopted on January 31, 1946, and the unitary reality of the Communist Party of Yugoslavia that lay behind the constitutional façade were readily recognizable by persons familiar with Soviet reality. Just as the 1936 Soviet ("Stalin") Constitution provided for autonomous republics within the republic, the RSFSR, dominated by the largest Soviet ethnic group, so the Yugoslav Constitution provided for autonomous provinces within the republic, Serbia, with a sizable fraction of the largest Yugoslav ethnic group. (Strictly speaking, the first postwar Yugoslav constitution established Vojvodina as an autonomous province and Kosovo-Metohija as an autonomous region; by 1963 Kosovo had achieved a constitutional status equal to Vojvodina, and in 1968 "Metohija" was dropped as a concession to the predominantly Albanian population of the region [Rusinow, 1977].) Similarly, the 1946 Constitution provided for other institutions familiar to Soviet students: a legislature with a Council of Nationalities, and a ministerial system with a mix of All-Union, Union-Republic, and Republic ministries. A quarter-century later, by contrast, expectations about the constitutional basis of federalism in Yugoslavia or of a monolithic hierarchical party behind the constitution based on a knowledge of the Soviet system would have provided little guidance in orienting oneself in the world of Yugoslav federalism. That was a world where, by the 1960s, the courts were being asked to rule on clashes between republic and federal law; where fast risers in the party, the Croatian Miko Tripalo, for instance, were leaving Belgrade and returning to Zagreb, the capital of Croatia, where the action was; where republic party congresses routinely took place before the congress of what from 1952 on was called the League of Yugoslav Communists (LCY); and where by 1970 the representative to the LCY, Milos Zanko, could be recalled for articulating a stance prevalent in Belgrade, but unacceptable to the republic party organization in Croatia.

The open borders policy and the genuinely federal character of the political system are two of the most unambiguous changes in the Yugoslav political system that developed in the aftermath of the Stalin-Tito break and prefigure much of what follows. It is my view that the Stalin-Tito break is crucial to an understanding of the political evolution of Yugoslavia. It fundamentally altered the operative Yugoslav international environment. That altered environment in turn provided a context conducive to shifts away from the Yugoslav elites' initial strategies concerning Yugoslavia's basic foreign policy orientation, its links to the international economy, its choice of political institutions, and the relations between regime and society. The result is that Yugoslavia ceased to be the kind of closed system it was before the Stalin-Tito split and became instead a relatively open system that, unlike the satellite model, is penetrated by multiple sources.

The implications of what I am proposing may become clearer if I make explicit what is being rejected. For instance, in contrast to Gavriel Ra'anan [1977, p. 9], I reject the idea that Yugoslavia is part of Eastern Europe, as we shall see in greater detail below. I also reject the view expressed by Richard Farkas [1975, p. 81] that "the degree of foreign political penetration into the domestic political affairs of Yugoslavia is negligible." Quite the contrary: as we shall see, the degree of foreign political penetration is considerable, and it is difficult to imagine how by the mid-1970s persons could claim otherwise. All too often, scholars, having rightfully concluded that Yugoslavia was not a satellite, often proceeded to analyze Yugoslav politics almost exclusively from the vantage point of the internal "keys" to Yugoslavia's political evolution: internationality relations, economic problems, the succession issue.

My approach stresses the value of asking the question "What difference does it make for a state's political evolution that it exists in an international environment as well as a domestic one?" A moment's reflection, however, suggests a number of major possible implications. One can readily imagine, indeed Harold Lasswell did so fifty years ago, that the external environment could affect the basic structure and goals of the state. One could imagine, too, that resources generated in the external environment can become political goods that are allocated by the political system; and that "domestic" issues are affected by the perceived consequences externally of particular domestic outcomes. Domestic groups might use actors in the external environment to shape the outcomes of political controversies. Indeed, actors in the external environment may actually participate in the ostensibly domestic political process, so that the international environment overlaps with either the domestic environment or the political system itself. Decisionmakers, finally, might make use of the international environment as a resource for implementing putatively domestic policies or as part of an overall development strategy. In the case of Yugoslavia, I argue that the answer is "all of the above."

In developing this argument, I focus on three central areas: one is perhaps the most traditional area of national-international linkages. I refer to the linkage between outputs occurring in the external realm resulting from domestic sources and processed by the political system, or, less ponderously, the domestic sources of foreign policy. How have Yugoslav elites answered over time the question as to what orientation Yugoslavia should manifest toward states or specific groups of states? What strategy, to use an almost unavoidable term in this context, of alignment should it pursue to maximize Yugoslav interests both internal and external? Beyond the question of national-international linkages, moreover, there are the equally important matters of international-national linkages. What ties are there between the external environment in which Yugoslavia operates, its basic foreign policy, and its domestic political institutions?

The second area of concern involves the way in which the external environment impinges on basic Yugoslav institutions and policy processes. At one level we shall be tracing the evolution of the approaches Yugoslav elites have adopted in asking, "How ought the country to be organized politically?" Does the institutionalized Leninist Party that served Tito so well in World War II and in resisting Stalin represent the preferred organizational strategy for ensuring national cohesion and resisting attempts by external forces to exert influences on Yugoslavia's domestic affairs? At another level, however, the task will be to describe how ties, real and potential, with the international environment influence the game of politics in Yugoslavia, and to suggest how choices about the country's orientation to the international environment may bear significantly on the nature of Yugoslav political processes.

A third area of attention involves the linkage between the international and Yugoslav economies and Yugoslav mass-elite relations. Here we are concerned to detail the political and economic consequences of openness by examining the ramifications for Yugoslavia of massive outflows of Yugoslav workers abroad.

The approach adopted in addressing these three sets of questions varies. Chapter 2, "Independence, Alignment Policies, and Yugoslav Self-Management," updates a story that has been told on several previous occasions. I invert the usual argument, however, and contend that self-management is a product of the complex of policies that came to be known as nonalignment rather than, as is the conventional wisdom, the reverse. In Chapter 3, I show how events or resources that are external in origin to Yugoslavia are mediated by Yugoslav policy processes. Again, much of the substantive basis for that chapter has been covered elsewhere; what is novel is the effort to apply an issue-area paradigm in a non-American setting as a way of illustrating the evolving Yugoslav rules of the game, and of relating that evolution to its external environment. Chapters 4 and 5 contain considerable data about the international mobility of citizens, most notably as guest workers in Western Europe, with which even the most conversant students of Yugoslavia are probably unfamiliar. As in the other substantive chapters, though, I am more concerned to recast the way we think about the impact of the open borders policy for the political evolution of Yugoslavia than in presenting new data about the workers' migration per se.

The answers to these three sets of questions in turn serve as the basis for the final chapter which addresses two issues. It considers the substantive implications of assessing international-national linkages for the study of the evolution of Yugoslav politics, and secondly it relates the approach to the understanding of Yugoslav political changes developed in this book to the broader study of comparative and world politics.

2

INDEPENDENCE, ALIGNMENT POLICIES, AND YUGOSLAV SELF-MANAGEMENT

A major dimension of an independent state's quest for security is the nature of its ties to other states. Since that is also a central element in what practitioners, analysts, and the attentive public have in mind when they think of a state's foreign policy, it is also the dimension of a state's relationship to the international environment that receives the greatest scrutiny. In this chapter I examine the evolving pattern of Yugoslavia's orientation to states or particular groups of states. Inevitably this entails a focus primarily on the evolving content of Yugoslav nonalignment. A major argument of the chapter is that by addressing communist Yugoslavia's orientation to states or groups of states, we move a long way to answering a host of other important questions concerning Yugoslav politics and policies as well. Among these are questions concerning the defining features of the Yugoslav political system, the degree and sources of external penetration, and the overall pattern of trade relations. These, in turn, relate to Yugoslavia's changing place in the international system and are a product partly of the Yugoslav elite's quest for regime security, system security, and "nation-state" security.

Such a quest, of course, presumes that a state is independently pursuing its own security goals, that it is, in communist jargon, pursuing "nationalist" goals, and not just subordinating its aspirations to the "proletarian internationalist" goals of the Soviet Union. This has been the case for Yugoslav communist elites ever since the second meeting of the Partisan-dominated Anti-Fascist Council of National Liberation (AVNOJ), in November 1943. At that meeting AVNOJ was declared " 'the supreme legislative and executive body of Yugoslavia' without the USSR having been informed in advance" [Johnson, 1972, p. 29].

ALIGNMENT WITH MOSCOW

A reason for Yugoslavia's persistently independent behavior is to be found in the manner by which Yugoslav communism came to power. Yugoslavia is what Zvi Gitelman has called an authentic rather than a derivative communist system: like the Soviets, the Yugoslavs came to power largely on their own.

This had immediate and evident consequences for Yugoslavia's relations with other states. The Yugoslavs signed a treaty of Mutual Aid, Friendship,

Economic and Cultural Mutual Cooperation with the Soviet Union on April 11, 1945. That treaty was but one of several similar bilateral treaties that Moscow signed with the European socialist states between 1943 and 1948. Tito greeted the signing as

> The most significant foreign policy act in the history of new Yugoslavia. This great historical act was enthusiastically greeted by all our peoples. This act has long and steadfastly been desired by all our peoples. But it is only now, twenty-six years after the establishment of old Yugoslavia, only after the great catastrophe which overcame our country in 1941, only after the peoples of Yugoslavia in the liberation struggle had taken their destinies into their own hands and removed anything that hindered the rapprochement with the brotherly Soviet nation—it is only after all this that finally the centuries-long aspirations of our peoples have been realized and an indestructible link established with the peoples of the Soviet Union, which will be the guarantee of our security and a great benefit for the development of our country [Tito, 1959, pp. 16-17, and cited in Mates, 1970, p. 189].

From such statements and acts it would be easy to envisage Yugoslavia compliantly following the Soviet lead in a fashion commensurate with the behavior of the states occupied by the Soviet army: evidence for such collaboration would be found in the early U.N. General Assembly behavior of Yugoslavia where in 1946, 1947, and 1948 Yugoslavia voted in agreement with the Soviet Union 95 percent, 97 percent, and 96 percent of the time, respectively (see Table 2.2).

There certainly is little question that Yugoslavia was aligned with the Soviet Union in these years, as Yugoslav accounts readily acknowledge. Like Mao's China, Tito's Yugoslavia "leaned to one side." Leo Mates [1972], the former Yugoslav Ambassador to the United States, in his study of *non*-alignment—the one word most associated with Yugoslav foreign policy in the Tito era—rightly calls the first section treating "the specific characteristics of Yugoslavia's international position after World War II" simply "alignment." He also rightly stresses that the alignment was voluntary, not coerced: "Yugoslavia voluntarily and with a full conviction of the rightness of her act, took the side of the Soviet Union and considered herself attached and aligned with it in its confrontation with its former allies from the West [1972, p. 177]. Throughout the 1945-1948 period, a major theme in Yugoslav behavior, internationally and domestically, was that it revealed its autonomy by being more Catholic than the Pope, to wit, more Stalinist than Stalin. The relevant illustration pertaining to Yugoslav alignment policies is that Yugoslavia proceeded to negotiate and sign its own set of bilateral treaties in several instances before the Soviet counterparts were signed, and well before the derivative East European states signed bilateral Friendship and Mutual Aid treaties with each other (see Table 2.1).

What needs to be stressed is that simultaneously Yugoslavia was aggressively pursuing its own particularist goals with or without Moscow's consent. These interests concerned Albania (where Yugoslavia had established a virtual satellite), Trieste, the nature of the Danube River regime, and the creation of a possible Balkan Federation involving Yugoslavia, Bulgaria, and Albania. Of these concerns, Yugoslav behavior concerning Trieste most vividly illustrates the vigor with which the Yugoslavs pursued their own claims and the mental set of the leadership that had just accomplished its own revolution. In the spring of 1945, the Yugoslavs were willing to risk war with the U.S. and Great Britain in order to claim territory given to Austria or Italy at Versailles with substantial Slavic populations and in particular Trieste itself. (Thirty years later, ordinary Yugoslavs would rejoice that these efforts had been unsuccessful since, had "we gotten Trieste, we would have to drive all the way to Milan to shop.") The Yugoslav leaders were, moreover, apparently surprised that in May 1945 the Soviet Union was not equally willing to risk confrontation over Trieste. Tito in his speech in Ljubljana (May 27, 1945), reacting to charges made by the Western press that he wanted Trieste for the Soviet Union, declared that "with the new Yugoslavia there is no brokering, nor is it for sale": "We demand that everyone shall be master in his own house. . . . We will no longer be dependent on anyone." At Versailles "some politicians . . . lightly gave

TABLE 2.1
Friendship and Mutual Aid Treaties

	Romania	Poland	Hungary
U.S.S.R.	2- 4-48	4-21-45	2-18-48
Yugoslavia	12-19-47	3-18-46	12- 8-47
Bulgaria	11-16-48	5-29-48	7-16-48
Czechoslovakia	7-21-48	3-10-47	4-16-49
Hungary	1-24-48	6-18-48	
Poland	1-26-49		

	Czechoslovakia	Bulgaria	Yugoslavia
U.S.S.R.	12-12-43	3-18-48	4-11-45
Yugoslavia	3- 9-46	11-27-47	
Bulgaria	4-23-48		

SOURCES: Brzezinski [1967], p. 110; Strbac [1975], p. 24.
NOTE: Albania signed Friendship and Mutual Aid treaties with Yugoslavia on July 9, 1946, and with Bulgaria on December 12, 1947.

crumbs to our country . . . but today is a different situation" [Tito, 1959, pp. 302-303].

The Soviet view of this statement we largely know from the subsequent Soviet-Yugoslav polemics in 1948 and these are demonstrably colored by the tenor of those times. In 1948, Moscow declared that "Since all other means were exhausted [in 1945], the Soviet Union had only one other method left for gaining Trieste for Yugoslavia—to start war with the Anglo-Americans over Trieste and take it by force" [Bass and Marbury, eds., 1959, p. 29]. We also, however, have a rather good sense of the Soviet reaction in 1945. It, too, was very sharp. In June 1945 Moscow instructed the Soviet Ambassador in Belgrade to "Tell Comrade Tito that if he should once again make such an attack on the Soviet Union, it will be necessary to answer him critically in the press and to disavow him." [*Pisma*, 1948, as cited in Strbac, 1975, p. 66].

In 1945 and even in 1948 the Yugoslavs evidenced the hubris, characteristic of successful power seizure, that led them to expect that the Soviet Union would support them completely against the British and Americans, even to the point of risking war over Trieste. (There is a nice analogue to Chinese expectations regarding Moscow's support in the Quemoy-Matsu conflict.) That hubris induced a kind of naïvete about Yugoslav foreign policy: the Yugoslavs believed that close alignment with the Soviet Union and the pursuit of specifically Yugoslav foreign policy concerns were compatible.

They were not. The years between 1945 and 1947 were ones of relative diversity in the world communist movement in comparison with the years after Yugoslavia was expelled from the Cominform in 1948. Nevertheless, from 1945 to 1947, Stalin was intent on imposing satellite status on Yugoslavia through the use of such traditional control mechanisms as joint stock companies, the appointment of Soviet advisers at strategic points in the governmental apparatus and economy, the penetration of and recruitment of spies and agents in the Yugoslav army, and by insisting on a special satrap-like status for the Soviet Ambassador.

It took quite a while for the Yugoslav leaders to come to regard the Soviet acts as threatening. When one reads the Yugoslav accounts, it is evident they viewed the introduction of advisers and joint stock companies, for instance, as a logical concomitant of the relation between the first socialist state, the Soviet Union, and Yugoslavia. (The Yugoslavs themselves extended similar "fraternal aid" to Albania.) What they were not prepared for was that espionage, exploitation, and the recruitment of agents among the Yugoslav citizenry would become commonplace. And they certainly did not expect that Stalin would demand, as he did on February 10, 1948, that Kardelj sign an agreement mandating consultation on foreign policy matters with the Soviet government.

Kardelj signed—though from then on relations between the two states deteriorated rapidly as the Yugoslavs rejected further demands from Stalin. Kardelj's words speak volumes about the Yugoslav leadership's expectations about the Soviet Union: "I was listening to . . . Molotov ordering 'sign this' and I was boiling with rage. Why should the whole thing be done in that manner? *The Yugoslav government was not against consultation* [with the Soviet Union] *on questions of foreign policy.* . . . The humiliation of it disgusted and perplexed me—it reminded me only of the dictates of the big powers to small and weak ones. I was wondering what to do, whether to sign or not. At last I decided to affix my signature" [Dedijer, 1953, p. 333, italics added].

As Stalin said to Bulgaria's Georgi Dimitrov concerning Soviet-Yugoslav relations, foreign policy "mistakes are not the issue: the issue is conceptions different from our own" [Dedijer, 1953, p. 327]. Stalin was bent on establishing a situation where "conceptions different from our own" would be precluded because the Yugoslavs would not be in a position to make "mistakes."

The famous Cominform resolution of June 28, 1948, anathematized the YCP by declaring it "outside the family of the fraternal Communist Parties, outside the united Communist front and consequently outside the ranks of the Information Bureau as a result of its leadership's anti-Party and anti-Soviet views, incompatible with Marxism-Leninism . . . their whole attitude and their refusal to attend the meeting of the Information Bureau" [Bass and Marbury, eds., 1959, pp. 44-45]. In so doing, the Cominform called on the "healthy elements" within the YCP "to compel their present leaders to recognize their mistakes openly and honestly and to rectify them," or failing this, "to replace them and to advance a new internationalist leadership of the Party." As Tito said in July 1948, this was "a call to civil war, a call to destroy our country," or in Adam Ulam's words, "The central point was: who [was] to have political power in Yugoslavia?" [1952, p. 107].

By seeking to oust Tito and penetrate the political and economic systems, Moscow threatened the regime security of the Yugoslav leadership, called into question the future capacity of the Yugoslavs themselves to mobilize and allocate resources—system security—as well as sought to undermine nation-state security [cf. Linden, 1982, pp. 157-159].

There were, we now know, rather sizable "healthy elements," more than the literature has conventionally depicted [Banac in Vucinich, ed., 1982]. At the federal level, the efforts by Moscow to mobilize opposition to Tito were largely unsuccessful, notwithstanding the long tradition of factionalism within the YCP, the YCP's subservience to the Soviet Union in the

17

Comintern years, and the fact that Moscow had "managed to penetrate the Yugoslav Communist party's highest councils; Andrija Hebrang and Sretan Vujovic regularly reported to the Kremlin." In the republics, too, the Cominform's efforts were also thwarted. "A group of highly placed Serbs in the Croatian Party from Lika . . . [opted] for the Cominform" [Shoup, 1968, p. 138], and the Montenegrin party organization had an unusually large number of pro-Soviet supporters: its rate of expulsions for Cominform sympathies was higher than that of any other republic. "During the summer and autumn of 1948 an entire UDB-a [secret police] division was on duty in Montenegro to suppress the growing Cominformist guerilla activity and prevent the flight of [Cominformists] to Albania" [Banac in Vucinich, ed., 1982, pp. 24-27]. Albania, Hungary, and Bulgaria endeavored with some success to exacerbate nationality tensions among the Yugoslav Albanians, Hungarians, and Macedonians.

Nevertheless, the leadership, moving with dispatch, sometimes with subtlety and often with brutality, managed to quell any internal disturbances. The YCP at all levels was brought into line, and the Yugoslav secret police, Aleksandar Rankovic revealed in 1951, arrested some 8,400 real and imagined Cominformists; again according to Rankovic, 47 percent of the arrests in 1949 were subsequently acknowledged to have been "unjustified" [Farrell, 1956, pp. 122-123]. An irony in all this is that while independence and alliance with Stalin's Soviet Union were incommensurate goals, the aping of the Soviet Union, its institutions and practices, contributed in no small measure to communist Yugoslavia's effective resistance to Stalin's pressures when push came to shove.

EXILE FROM EASTERN EUROPE

The Soviet split with Yugoslavia had few obvious immediate consequences for Yugoslav foreign policy. Relations with the West did not improve substantially in the immediate aftermath of the Cominform attack, and the Yugoslavs continued to inveigh against the dangers of Anglo-American imperialism. (An important counter-instance related to Yugoslav-American relations, however, was the United States' decision in July 1948 to unfreeze certain Yugoslav assets, in particular some $47,000,000 worth of gold, an act which Frank G. Wisner, Deputy Assistant Secretary of State depicted to Averill Harriman as a "very 'timely' development" [U. S. Department of State, 1974, p. 1097].)

Nor is it appropriate to date the notion of nonalignment with the immediate aftermath of the Cominform attack. "At that time Yugoslavia's policy of independence could not be described as nonalignment, but rather as a policy of isolation and acceptance of the challenge from all the great powers'' [Mates, 1972, p. 205]. Rather, Yugoslavia's initial position in the immediate aftermath of the break was one in which its relations were bad with all the major powers; the hope persisted for a reconciliation with Stalin and the Soviet Union. Throughout 1948, despite Soviet invective, the Yugoslavs continued to evince their public loyalty to the Soviet Union and to Stalin: Stalin's sixty-ninth birthday in December 1948 was greeted with

> There are no kinds of difficulties, no matter which side they come from, that cannot be set aside from the road to the building of socialism and the struggle against imperialism, and on that road we must always keep before our eyes the enormous experience of the USSR which is elaborated in the works of Stalin.
> Long live the leader of progressive mankind, Joseph Vissarionovich Stalin [*Borba*, December 21, 1948, in Rubinstein, 1970, p. 8].

In part, the Yugoslav leaders were making such utterances in order to make it easier for Yugoslav communists to become convinced that one could be loyal to Tito and still be a good communist, and that it was only Stalin's intransigence that was responsible for the clash. They also, however, continued to have that blend of self-righteousness and self-assurance that seems to come with successful power seizure: there were no barriers that communists could not storm, even ones erected by Stalin. Without that mental set in view, it is difficult to explain why, as they did, the Yugoslavs *accelerated* the pace of collectivization after the Cominform attack.

Moreover, key figures in the Yugoslav elite continued to regard Yugoslavia as one of the Peoples' Democracies, that it *"like other countries* of the Peoples' Democracies, can exist and develop only . . . by remaining in fraternal union with the USSR and the other Peoples' Democracies, and by developing further that union'' [*Borba*, July 20, 1948, in Rubinstein, 1970, p. 5; italics added]. Louis Adamic [1952, p. 260] writes that for a full year Tito and Kardelj continued to manifest ''vestiges of the old hope-against-hope sentiment'' for a reconciliation with Stalin. The aspiration for some form of association with the European socialist states—but not the idea that socialist construction in Yugoslavia required remaining in ''fraternal union with the USSR''—was to persist at least until the Soviet invasion of Hungary in November 1956. There was, in the first year after the Cominform attack, little awareness that Yugoslavia was one of the first real beneficiaries of loose bipolarity, and nothing to suggest a conscious effort to define Yugoslavia as outside the East European hierarchical regional system.

The change in Yugoslavia's position in the international system was, however, taking place and taking place rapidly, as a result of Soviet actions. The heavy concentration of trade with the East that had been a logical accompaniment to communist power seizure was severed abruptly by a Soviet blockade. As with most blockades that lack great-power consensus, the Soviet blockade failed. Rather than bringing down the Yugoslav leadership, the blockade facilitated a major redirection in Yugoslav trade toward the West. In 1947, for instance, Yugoslavia imported more from the Soviet Union than it did from the U.S., Italy, Great Britain, France, and Austria combined. By 1948, Yugoslavia was importing more from each of those countries than from the Soviet Union, and for four years, trade between Yugoslavia and the Peoples' Democracies ceased completely [Tomasevich in Vucinich, ed., 1982, pp. 105-106].

Further evidence of Yugoslav isolation quickly became manifest. Border incidents and troop movements multiplied. Yugoslav accounts assert that there were almost 1500 border incidents with Hungary, Romania, and Bulgaria in 1948, 1949, and 1950. In June 1949, a year after the Cominform attack, the Soviet Union made it plain that Moscow would no longer support Yugoslavia's territorial claims in the ethnically mixed zones on the latter's western borders, this time with Austria. Likewise, Moscow showed that in its calculus Yugoslavia was no longer part of Eastern Europe by failing to involve it in the creation (largely on paper) in January 1949 of a Council for Mutual Economic Assistance—a symbolic riposte to the Marshall Plan. The most telling act, perhaps, occurred in September 1949 when Moscow canceled the Soviet-Yugoslav Treaty of Friendship and Mutual Assistance. The bilateral treaties had been the basis, institutionally, for establishing relations between the communist states and the rest of the world. Hence, to abrogate that treaty was to italicize the notion that in a two-camp world, Yugoslavia was in the wrong camp. As a Soviet diplomatic note (August 18, 1949) put it, "The present government of Yugoslavia [is] not . . . a friend or ally, but . . . an enemy" [*White Book*, 1951, p. 93; also Strbac, 1975, pp. 97-109].

Furthermore, Moscow took the stance that the successful U.S. effort in the fall of 1949 to accord Yugoslavia a nonpermanent seat on the U.N. Security Council was an act of bad faith not only because it violated a gentlemen's agreement but, more to the point, because it violated the United Nations Charter which provided for the equitable *geographical* distribution of the nonpermanent members of the Security Council. In Moscow's eyes, and in the obvious ways one might operationalize the boundaries between Eastern Europe as a regional system and the rest of the world—trade flows and institutional membership, for instance—Yugoslavia was no longer part of Eastern Europe.

Thus the argument that there was a dramatic redirection of Yugoslav foreign and domestic policy that flowed from the Cominform clash is not a mechanical, action-reaction one. The impact of the changed international environment on Yugoslav behavior could be felt only as mediated by changed perceptions on the part of the Yugoslav leadership, and as those changed perceptions were legitimated by explanations cast in doctrinal terms.

Toward Nonalignment

This is in fact what happened. The period during which the Yugoslav leaders continued to behave as though reality had not changed—that Yugoslavia's relationship to Eastern Europe had not been altered drastically—was relatively brief. Quite quickly they abandoned the two-camp thesis and declared, in Mose Pijade's words, that "There is no justification at all for the view that small nations must jump into the mouth of this or that shark. If that were a social law, there would not today be any small states" [*Borba*, July 9, 1949, as cited in Rubinstein, 1970, p. 14].

As that insight permeated the consciousness of the Yugoslav leaders, several of the major strands in Yugoslav foreign policy, that when woven together come to constitute constant features of nonalignment, begin to appear. This is not to date a fully articulated commitment to, or doctrine of, nonalignment to 1949. It is, however, to assert that in order to depict the trends that, taken together, characterize Titoist foreign policy for a quarter-century from the mid-1950s until his death in 1980, one needs to understand the changes in thinking and behavior that occurred between 1949 and 1955. With those changes in mind, moreover, one can portray Yugoslav foreign policy in rather broad strokes for the 1960s and 1970s while still achieving an appropriate sense of the persisting themes in Yugoslav behavior and thinking, particularly since that story has been well told by Rubinstein [1970], Mates [1972], Rusinow [1977], and Wilson [1979].

One central aspect of nonalignment as an overarching policy is the clear preference for the global south over the global east or west. For this to occur required a major rethinking of the international behavior of the Soviet Union and the United States and of the largely postcolonial states of Africa and Asia. This occurred between 1949 and 1955.

In 1948 Yugoslav statements about what came to be known as the Third World were colored by the kinds of attitudes toward the "national bourgeoisie" traditionally associated with leftist strands in communist thinking. Just as Krishna Menon, for the Russians, was a lackey of Anglo-American imperialism, the Yugoslavs saw Nehru as fronting for the interests of Indian reaction and British imperialism. By 1950-1951, Yugoslav elites were well launched toward a major reassessment of Africa and Asia, and India in particular. While continuing to stress the dependence implicit in economic ties to the erstwhile metropoles, the Yugoslavs clearly recognized that these states were independent forces and increasingly began to perceive them as potential allies. By March 1953, when Stalin died, the Yugoslavs were cultivating close ties with Ethiopia, Burma, and India and had begun to identify themselves with Third World socialism (not communism) rather than "Cominformism" or "capitalism" [Johnson, 1972, Rubinstein, 1970, and Mates, 1970]. On his return from a trip to India in late 1954 and early 1955, Tito described the uncommitted states as "true allies and . . . our greatest friends" [as cited in Rubinstein, 1970 p. 64], thus setting the stage for the July 1956 Brioni meeting of Tito, Nasser, and Nehru, a meeting which symbolized the raising of nonalignment to the level of state policy.

For that to occur, however, also required the Yugoslavs to adjust their views of both the United States and the Soviet Union, and for them to conclude definitively that there were no acceptable terms under which they could once again be part of Eastern Europe. As Marxist-Leninists, the Yugoslavs had to confront doctrinally the issue of Soviet foreign policy behavior. Since for Marxists foreign policy is a product of a state's political system, the issue was: How could Stalin's hegemonial policies be possible? Dusan Bilandzic has nicely put the issue as it was viewed by the Yugoslavs: "Either there exist real Communists and true socialism in the USSR—in which case the Soviet Communist Party is right in its clash with the CPY— or else Socialism there is deformed and Communists there are no longer Communists, in which case the CPY is the true Marxist Party and Stalin and the CPSU leadership no longer stand on the true socialist positions" [Bilandzic, 1969, pp. 45f.; cited in Rusinow, 1977, p. 46].

It will not surprise readers to learn that for those Yugoslavs who opted for Tito against the Cominform the answer was that socialism in the U.S.S.R. was deformed. As a result, one had to distinguish socialism in Yugoslavia, "state capitalism" in the Soviet Union, and capitalism in the West [Johnson, 1972]. Against that backdrop, there was a rationale for improving relations with the West. As Johnson writes, "It reassured the CPY—although not completely successfully—that, in cooperating with the United States and other Western powers against the Soviet Union, Yugoslavia was not aiding imperialism but was opposing the threat of Stalinist imperialism in a world where socialism had already won its world-historical victory over capitalism" [1972, p. 139].

The improvement in relations with the West did not happen overnight. Rather the anti-imperialist rhetoric persisted for at least a year. Public evidence of tangible changes in relations between Yugoslavia and the U.S. and the United Kingdom did become apparent in September 1949. At that juncture the U.S. extended the Yugoslavs a 20 million dollar loan. (In fact, however, both the Anglo-Americans and the Yugoslavs had signaled an interest in improved relations earlier: hence, the U.S. release of Yugoslav gold and the Yugoslav undertaking to diminish and then sever aid to the Greek communists.) Slightly more than a year after the first loan, the Yugoslavs formally requested U.S. aid; on November 29, 1950 (the Yugoslav national holiday), President Harry S. Truman asked Congress to endorse the Yugoslav Emergency Relief Act; that act was signed a month later; and in January 1951 the U.S. and Yugoslavia signed an agreement on the supplies to be furnished under the law. No study focusing on the theme of international-national linkages would be complete without taking note of Section 6, Article II of that agreement which, as Tomasevich notes [in Vucinich, ed., 1982, p. 110],

> imposed certain, though unspecified, obligations on the Yugoslav government with regard to its internal economic policies: "The government of the Federal People's Republic of Yugoslavia will take all appropriate economic measures to reduce its relief needs, to encourage increased production and distribution of foodstuffs within Yugoslavia, and to lessen the danger of future conditions of food shortage similar to the present emergency." What the United States government had in mind here was, undoubtedly, Yugoslav policies in regard to agriculture, such as compulsory deliveries, discriminatory prices, confiscatory taxation, and attempted collectivization. . . .

Given the 1950 drought and the catastrophic drop in agricultural output, it was not surprising that Yugoslavia decided to abandon collectivization in the early 1950s; U.S. aid enhanced the likelihood that such a decision would be reached.

Moreover, between 1950 and 1954, U.S. assistance involved both economic and military aid [U.S. Agency for International Development, 1961]. This included the establishment of a Military Assistance Advisory Group in Belgrade, an arrangement which was followed in early 1953 by a Treaty of Friendship and Cooperation with Turkey and Greece, and the Balkan Pact, signed at Bled on August 9, 1954. The latter, as Rusinow [1977, p. 46] notes, "defined an act of aggression against one as an act of aggression against all, created a permanent secretariat for collaboration, and called for continuing military staff discussions and regular meetings of the three foreign ministers." Mates, in fact, states that "A discreet pressure was on all the time to bring Yugoslavia a little closer to the Western countries. In the end it was even pointed out that Yugoslavia's interests, her independence, integrity and frontiers would best be safeguarded if she were to join the North Atlantic Pact" [1972, p. 207].

Ironically, however, the Balkan Pact was virtually moribund at birth. Just when Yugoslavia seemed closest formally to a reversal of alliances, relations with Moscow had begun to improve with Stalin's death, Khrushchev's rise, and the ouster of Djilas in Yugoslavia. Stalin's death and the subsequent decompression in the Soviet Union rekindled the persistent hope among the Yugoslav leadership for some sort of special relationship with Eastern Europe.

Over Molotov's strenuous objections, Khrushchev gave Tito the opportunity he sought by coming to Belgrade in 1955 and recognizing, in the June 2 Belgrade Declaration, that "for the purpose of strengthening confidence and cooperation between the peoples" of the Soviet Union and Yugoslavia, each state affirms its "respect for the sovereignty, independence, integrity, and equality of states in their relations with each other" and pledges its "observance of the principles of mutual respect and noninterference in internal affairs for any reason": "Questions of the internal structure, of different social systems, and of different ways of advancing to socialism are exclusively a matter for the peoples of the individual countries" [*Review of International Affairs*, 1955].

Khrushchev's efforts found a ready response in Belgrade. Tito welcomed the opportunity to have a major voice in matters pertaining to Eastern Europe. Yugoslavia acquired a special favored status in Soviet eyes, national communism seemed to be legitimated and the heretic triumphant. The special relationship, however, lasted only until the second Soviet intervention in Hungary in November 1956. The Yugoslavs, although they provided asylum for Imre Nagy, acquiesced in the Soviet intervention in Hungary where the Hungarian Workers' Party had collapsed, multiparty rule had been restored, and neutrality declared. The intervention, the Yugoslavs asserted, was a "lesser evil" necessary to ensure "the preservation of socialism in Hungary." The degree of Yugoslav support, when combined with the granting of asylum for Nagy, was insufficient for Moscow, and an almost instantaneous reversal in Soviet-Yugoslav relations occurred. On the night of November 2-3, Khrushchev and Malenkov spent from 7 P.M. to 5 A.M. consulting with Tito, during which time Tito endorsed the Soviet intervention. By November 7 the Soviet leadership informed the Yugoslav Ambassador to Moscow, Veljko Micunovic, that, in the latter's words, "there is no longer a special relationship between us, as there was only three days ago," a message which Moscow had conveyed more explicitly two days before in Budapest where "The Russians, unprovoked by anybody, opened fire from machine guns and killed one of our diplomats in the embassy. . . . A bomb is supposed to have exploded in the immediate proximity of the Soviet tanks which were maintaining a blockade of our embassy, and it was only then that the Russian tanks opened fire 'in the direction from which they had been threatened,' i.e., at the Yugoslav embassy building" [Micunovic, 1980, pp. 151-152].

THE Hungarian revolution was a watershed in Soviet-Yugoslav relations. After it, the Yugoslav leadership, and Tito in particular, made it clear that future relations with the Soviet Union would be premised on the assumption that Yugoslavia was not part of Eastern Europe. Concretely, this implied that Yugoslavia would reject full membership in either the Warsaw Treaty Organization or Comecon and would not accede to obligatory bilateral consultative ties with the CPSU. Without ever abandoning completely the notion that Yugoslavia had a role to play in Eastern Europe, but from the outside, Tito turned consciously to the global south and to an explicitly extra-bloc policy, institutional and doctrinal expression for which was found in the analysis contained in the League of Yugoslav Communists' Program adopted in 1958.

A second major component of nonalignment prefigured in the years between 1949 and 1955 was its global rather than regional orientation to relations among states. This was revealed both with respect to domain and, in terms of identification, with respect to international institutions and norms. There were several dimensions to this development regarding nonalignment during the years following the Cominform attack. In part, in the early 1950s, it flowed from the Yugoslavs' tendency to take themselves seriously and to view themselves as the doctrinal spokesmen for socialism as a world process against the forces of capitalism and state capitalism. This tendency was reinforced in the early 1950s as the Yugoslavs began to identify themselves with socialism outside Europe.

A much more specific initial impetus prompting a concern for universal principles stemmed from the Yugoslav leaders' desire to secure their own boundaries from threats emanating from Cominform states. That concern quickly dominated Yugoslav interest in providing fraternal aid to Greek communists, to whom the Yugoslavs had provided aid and sanctuary since the end of World War II. By October 1948, Yugoslav aid had diminished. In May 1949 Tito told Fitzroy Maclean that "Greek guerillas would not be allowed to return to Greece after fleeing to Yugoslavia" and that "no other help would be given the Greek insurgents" [Pappas in Vucinich, ed., 1982, p. 224; also U.S. Department of State, 1974].

Likewise what had been, in the first years after World War II, the intense desire of the Yugoslav leaders to expand the confines of Yugoslavia, whether through a Balkan confederation or the acquisition of irridenta, gave way after 1949 to the desire to hold on to what they had. The reason for these more modest aspirations—aspirations far more readily expressed in universalist symbols—was the evidence of the seriousness of the Soviet threat. Most accounts agree that the Soviet Union's withdrawal of support for the Yugoslavs in June 1949 on the question of the Carinthian region along the Austrian-Yugoslav border disabused the Yugoslavs of the hope that a short-run reconciliation was possible with the Soviet Union. It was, however, the ominous threat in August 1949 that the Soviet government would "be compelled to resort to other more effective means . . . for the protection of the rights and interests of Soviet citizens in Yugoslavia" [*White Book,* 1951, p. 126] to prevent the Yugoslavs from maltreating Yugoslav "White Guard" Russians, many of whom had Soviet citizenship, which produced the greatest anxiety among the Yugoslav leadership for the security of the extant borders.

Against the backdrop of Soviet hostility, the territorial status quo, even with respect to Trieste, became an acceptable outcome by the early 1950s. Tito formally endorsed negotiation in 1952. Italy's *de facto* control of Zone A including Trieste and Yugoslavia's control over Zone B were recognized in the 1954 London Agreement between the U.S., Great Britain, Italy, and Yugoslavia. (Twenty years later in 1975 the *de jure* issue of sovereignty was finally resolved.)

Yugoslavia's newly found concern to maintain the territorial status quo dovetailed with its discovery of the United Nations. The Yugoslavs soon found that the U.N. and its agencies, the International Monetary Fund, UNESCO, and SUNFED, were potential sources of significant symbolic and tangible goods. Moreover, even during the period of American dominance of the General Assembly, the United Nations had the distinct advantage of being a theoretically universal, not regional or particularistic, organization. As such it was an appropriate forum for disputing the proposition that, as Kardelj expressed it in the fall of 1950, "Mankind must today choose between domination by one or another great power"; he went on to state his preference for "a world of free and equal nations, for democratic relations among nations, against interference from outside in the internal affairs of the nations and for an all-round peaceable cooperation of peoples on the basis of equality" [Mates, 1972, pp. 208-209].

The United Nations also was a vehicle for supporting efforts to thwart challenges to the territorial status quo and to a regime's security in noncolonial settings. Yugoslavia's first oportunity to demonstrate it had absorbed that insight occurred in the summer of 1950 when it supported the Uniting for Peace Resolution, legitimating the American response under the U.N. banner to the North Korean invasion of South Korea. The U.S.-U.N. action, it should be noted, may have deterred a Soviet-led invasion of Yugoslavia in 1951. Bela Kiraly, who commanded the Hungarian infantry from 1948 to 1951 and who was well versed in the planned role of the Hungarian army in such an invasion, states as his "firm belief" that U.S.-U.N. action "convinced Stalin . . . that in case of aggression against Yugoslavia Soviet troops might clash head-on with American troops there" [Kiraly in Vucinich, ed., 1982, pp. 286-287]. The Yugoslav invocation of universal symbols was a natural response to an international environment where proletarian internationalism did not imply Soviet support for Yugoslav territorial ambitions, and instead implied a Soviet determination of whether and when socialism was endangered.

The third major strand in the reorientation in Yugoslav relations toward the international environment involved the tie between Yugoslavia's foreign policy and its domestic political system. The Yugoslav leadership needed, first of all, to hold a diverse coalition together. In addition, it was both desirable and necessary to distinguish Yugoslavia from the Soviet Union without giving proof to Cominform charges that Yugoslavia had become a lackey of Anglo-American imperialism. (We have Tito's testimony that the acceptance of military aid from the U.S. posed genuine difficulties for "some comrades.") Rubenstein has developed nicely the case that a stance which entailed alignment with neither East nor West and which depicted ties with the global south as not constituting a third bloc—i.e., nonalignment— had the strong merit of being minimally acceptable to all members of the domestic coalition and thus "appropriate to the satisfaction of internal political requirements, and to the national purpose of ending Yugoslavia's diplomatic isolation and affording it an important international role" [1970, p. 72]. This was, for the majority of the leadership, far preferable to Djilas' views. "Had Djilas' new foreign policy been adopted," a republic party official told Rubinstein, Yugoslavia would have developed "into a two-Party system, along the lines of British Parliamentary democracy" resulting "in a much closer association with the Western camp [and] a dangerous splintering of the Party" [p. 73].

I believe this argument should be taken further. The clash with Djilas notwithstanding, what all the Yugoslav leaders—Tito, Bakaric, Kardelj, Rankovic, Boris Kedric, and Djilas—were doing in the early 1950s was looking for ways to mark Yugoslav communism off from the Soviet model. The "gimmick," as one astute Yugoslav expressed it to me, which they found was workers' control through self-management. Out of self-management, moreover, flowed several core doctrinal notions and a general premise, i.e., to replace the internal mobilization strategy prevalent between 1946 and 1949 with a more conciliatory policy toward society. During the brief but highly fertile period from 1949 through the Sixth Congress in 1952, much of what came to be thought of as Titoism emerged, all of it closely linked conceptually to self-management. The command economy with mandatory planning was replaced by indicative planning and market socialism, and the vanguard role of the YCP was abandoned. Instead, the League of Yugoslav Communists (LCY), as the party has been called since 1952, was mandated to serve as "an ideological and political leading force" largely separate from day-in, day-out policy implementation until such time when it withered away. Less directly related to self-management, but clearly tied to efforts to strengthen the regime's support at home and in the West, and part of

27

the overall pattern of devolution of power, was the decollectivization of agriculture. Taken together, self-management, the party's transformation into a "league of communists," market socialism, and private agriculture constitute the core of Yugoslavia's self-managing socialism.

The formulation usually articulated by Yugoslavs and Westerners, namely that nonalignment is an extension of self-management, is correct in important respects. It is even more appropriate, however, to view *self-management as an outgrowth of nonalignment*, or more exactly, out of the foreign policy trends which are subsumed by the rubric nonalignment when the latter becomes the keystone of Yugoslav foreign policy in the mid-1950s. The primacy of foreign policy considerations [see Tarazoulo in Vucinich, ed., 1982] seems overwhelming: to play a global role and differentiate Yugoslavia from the Soviet Union and the United States pointed directly to nonalignment. The domestic expression of those aspirations was self-managing socialism.

NONALIGNMENT AND THE INTERNATIONAL SYSTEM

Nonalignment has been the keystone of Yugoslavia's foreign policy since the mid-1950s. Until Tito's death at least, the three strands that emerged in the years from 1949 to 1955 persisted. The tie between domestic and foreign policy was made more complete by writing principles intrinsic to nonalignment into the Constitution of 1974. Part of the rationale—there were very likely other reasons as well—for excluding persons from the ruling coalition was that they were excessively pro-Western (hence the ouster of Stane Kavcic in 1972) or excessively pro-Soviet (as was implied of Aleksandar Rankovic in 1966). Such people, it was suggested, not only sought to bring Yugoslavia closer to the West or the East, but wished to alter Yugoslav institutions after the fashion of the West or East. Thus, in the ouster of Kavcic it was made clear that while part of the justification of his removal [Kardelj in *Borba*, September 22, 1972] was that an excessively close link to Europe was unacceptable to Moscow, it was also made known that his ouster was prompted by his ostensible support for "a two-party system and a parliament" [Jure Bilic in *Politika*, December 3, 1976].

Certainly the global character of Yugoslavia's nonalignment policy was evident in the incessant parade of meetings dating from the July 1956 meeting with Nasser and Nehru in Brioni up to Tito's incapacitation in late 1979 and in the far-flung scope of Yugoslav diplomatic activities. Almost certainly, the globalism contributed to Tito's legitimacy domestically, even though it also produced some resentment, in any event, in Slovenia.

The globalism was inspired by other motivations, however, that were less specific to Tito. There was the continuing desire to mark Yugoslavia off from East and West. More concretely, there was the important instrumental need, characteristic of independent small states generally, to defend principles of universal validity lest particularistic rationales be employed to legitimate hegemonic behavior by the more powerful.

The basis for these concerns was underscored by Soviet behavior after Hungary. The Yugoslavs viewed the Soviet intervention there as legitimate since socialism, as Yugoslavia defined the term, was in danger. The Soviet invasion of Czechoslovakia was more ominous and threatening. The Yugoslavs now realized that in Eastern Europe it was Moscow who would decide whether and when socialism was in danger. For the Yugoslavs, the changes in 1968 in Czechoslovakia were truly in the direction of a socialism with a human face: the Prague Spring found much of its inspiration in Yugoslav market socialism and was demonstrably supported by Tito. The Soviet action in Czechoslovakia convinced the Yugoslavs that the main danger to Yugoslav security stemmed from the Soviet Union and reconfirmed the wisdom of being a part of the international system rather than a part of Eastern Europe—where the norms of socialist international relations (to wit, proletarian internationalism with its doctrinally legitimated justification for Soviet intervention) obtained. Unfortunately for Yugoslavia, the emergence of the Soviet Union, for the first time really, as a world power with genuinely global force projection capabilities has called into question whether in Soviet minds the world has become, so to speak, Eastern Europe. Specifically, in its direct relations toward Yugoslavia, Moscow's behavior has been largely correct and nonthreatening—the primary qualification to this generalization being Brezhnev's offer of assistance to Tito during the 1971 Croatian crisis [Tito in *Borba*, December 19, 1971; Micunovic in *NIN*, August 22, 1982, pp. 51-52]. Nevertheless, its behavior elsewhere has called into question whether Moscow will live up to the commitments made in 1955 and again in 1976 to base its relations with Yugoslavia on the norms for the international system [Zimmerman in Terry, ed., 1984].

At the verbal level the issue is whether the Soviet Union will show, in the words of the Belgrade Declaration, "respect for the sovereignty, independence, integrity, and equality of states in their relations with each other" and therefore not interfere in Yugoslav internal affairs inasmuch as "questions of the internal structure, of different social systems, and of different ways of advancing to socialism are exclusively a matter for the peoples of the individual countries." Equally plausibly, the operative rhetoric may be to answer affirmatively, as did the Soviet journal *New Times* in 1980, the questions "What is the international solidarity of revolutionaries? . . . Does it consist, under justified, extraordinary conditions, in rendering material aid including military aid, all the more so when it is a case of blatant, massive outside intervention?" [No. 3, 1980, p. 10].

At the level of Soviet behavior the issue has been posed explicitly by two events in the late 1970s, each of which involved threats to communist non-aligned states. The Soviet-supported Vietnamese invasion of Kampuchea provoked Yugoslav fears that the Vietnamese proxy invasion of a nona-ligned communist state could serve as a precedent for acts that might endan-ger the security of other countries, and warned that ''armed confrontations between nonaligned and socialist countries reflect negatively on both the strength and the prestige of the nonaligned movement'' [*Vecernji list*, Jan-uary 6-7, 1979, as reported in *Yearbook of International Communist Af-fairs*, 1980, p. 102]. (The Soviet response was gratuitously threatening: *TASS* observed that the Vietnamese assistance was analogous to the assist-ance rendered Yugoslavia in 1944 by the Soviet Red Army.)

The Soviet invasion of Afghanistan in December 1979 was even more ominous. Whereas the Vietnamese invasion of Kampuchea kindled fears of the unleashing of Bulgaria on Yugoslavia, the Soviet action in Afghanistan bespoke the real possibility that the U.S.S.R. itself might intervene in some other nonaligned socialist country, e.g., Yugoslavia. The invasion of Af-ghanistan was described as the first such Soviet action ''outside the coun-tries of the so-called socialist community'': ''It is this which is the most worrying aspect, and which leads one to the notion that the action in Af-ghanistan has broken the ice for similar moves in some other country, which, like Afghanistan, does not belong to any military alliance'' [Milika Sundic cited in Stankovic, 1980, p. 3]. Small wonder, therefore, that Yu-goslavia should stress so the universal characteristics of norms for relations between states, or that Yugoslavia should have taken the lead, both in inter-national forums and in its own media, in condemning Soviet behavior which seemed to portend that the U.S.S.R. might act outside Eastern Europe as it does within the East European hierarchical regional system.

Likewise, the Yugoslav preference for the global south prevailed throughout the quarter-century from 1956 to 1980, however relations with particular states may have fluctuated. One could demonstrate this by a de-tailed chronicling of Tito's peregrinations or by depicting his and Yugo-slavia's roles at various meetings of the nonaligned—beginning, signifi-cantly, with the Belgrade Conference of the Nonaligned in 1961 and extending through the Havana meeting in 1979 and the post-Tito meeting in New Delhi [Mates, 1972; *Jugoslavija u svetu*, 1970; *Medjunarodni odnosi i vanjska politika socijalisticke Jugoslavije*, 1979]. A less tedious exercise, which makes the same point, is to examine aggregate United Nations Gen-eral Assembly voting patterns over an extended period (see Table 2.2; for more specific analyses of particular key votes, see Nord, 1974).

An immediately obvious point with respect to Yugoslavia that emerges from these data is how discrepant its votes are with those of the United

TABLE 2.2
Voting Convergence in the U.N. General Assembly in Percentages

	Yugoslavia and U.S.S.R.	Yugoslavia and India	Yugoslavia and Romania	Yugoslavia and U.S.	U.S.S.R. and India	U.S.S.R. and Romania	U.S.S.R. and Poland
1946	.95	.44	NA	.23	.47	NA	.84
1947	.97	.69	NA	.19	.69	NA	.97
1948	.96	.41	NA	.11	.41	NA	.95
1949	.79	.34	NA	.24	.40	NA	1.0
1950	.52	.72	NA	.42	.40	NA	1.0
1951	.43	.43	NA	.43	.57	NA	1.0
1952	.49	.60	NA	.39	.41	NA	.99
1953	.77	.85	NA	.42	.73	NA	1.0
1954	.68	.74	NA	.29	.65	NA	1.0
1955	.84	.89	.50	.38	.81	1.0	1.0
1956	.75	.71	.71	.39	.57	.93	.96
1957	.73	.85	.73	.35	.65	1.0	1.0
1958	.77	.87	.77	.42	.68	1.0	1.0
1959	.77	.73	.77	.20	.64	1.0	.98
1960	.83	.92	.83	.10	.75	1.0	1.0
1961	.93	.72	.71	.27	.60	.98	.98
1962	.80	.64	.80	.20	.55	1.0	1.0
1963	.69	.90	.72	.28	.66	.97	1.0
1964	NA	NA	NA	NA	NA	NA	NA
1965	.79	.81	.76	.29	.74	.93	1.0
1966	.87	.76	.83	.24	.69	.96	1.0
1967	.85	.85	.85	.13	.74	.90	.97
1968	.67	.85	.76	.25	.54	.87	.98
1969	.77	.82	.82	.27	.66	.73	1.0
1970	.70	.85	.79	.24	.61	.84	.94
1971	.70	.90	.80	.37	.71	.83	.99
1972	.62	.88	.84	.40	.63	.75	.97
1973	.70	.88	.82	.32	.69	.72	.98
1974	.71	.75	.80	.25	.57	.76	1.0
1975	.75	.92	.81	.31	.71	.69	.99
1976	.71	.94	.87	.24	.71	.80	.94
1977	.72	.98	.90	.38	.71	.74	.98
1978	.63	.92	.85	.39	.59	.65	.92
1979	.67	.88	.87	.27	.65	.67	.95
1980	.69	.86	.82	.22	.68	.71	.96
1981	.76	.86	.83	.14	.75	.77	.98

SOURCE: Interuniversity Consortium for Political and Social Research, Archive.

States. Given the strong anticolonialist thrust implied by Yugoslavia's ties to the Third World, it could hardly be otherwise. This is, however, easily subject to misinterpretation. Small Western allies like the Netherlands, and European industrial neutrals, e.g., Sweden and Austria, do not vote with the United States very often either. In 1981, for instance, both Sweden's and Austria's votes converged with those of the U.S. only 31 percent of the time. Equally obvious is the difference between the satellite status of Poland

31

throughout the postwar period and Yugoslavia. (The successful effort of the Romanians to disengage themselves somewhat from Eastern Europe and to assert the claim that they are both a developing and a socialist country is also readily apparent, as is the strong parallelism in recent Romanian and Yugoslav voting.) A more interesting point is that, after 1956, the tendency has been for the Yugoslavs to vote more with India than with the Soviet Union. Indeed, the trend seems to be in the direction of greater cohesion with India, whereas the proportion of times the Yugoslav and Soviet votes converge remains basically constant.

Beyond these three strands, moreover, there were three other elements that were integral to nonalignment as it took shape during the post-1956 period. One was the effort, within the overall framework of participation in the global international division of labor, to balance trade patterns in such a way as to encourage trade with the global south and to avoid the kinds of dependency relationships that Marxists and others have seen to flow from high trade concentration. This has not been an unmitigated success. There is, for some Yugoslav firms, an economic basis for political ties to the Third World, but as an examination of Yugoslav trade trends reveals (see Table 2.3,) the Third World remains the smallest of the "three thirds" with respect both to Yugoslav exports and imports. There was a steady trend in the 1970s away from trade with the West and to much closer economic relations with the East (see Table 2.3)—a trend that was partly driven, at least initially in the early 1970s, by political considerations. In the aftermath of the 1971 Croatian nationalist outbursts, Tito was fearful that the forces of "technocratism and anarcho-liberalism" had become excessively powerful, especially in the republic party organizations and related this in part to the country's trade relations with Western Europe. (Much the larger share of the explanation for the shift must be seen in global macroeconomic phenomena: the OPEC-induced global rise in oil prices, Western stagflation, Yugoslav oil purchases from the Soviet Union.) The result, however, by the end of Tito's life did not produce a situation in which Yugoslavia was less dependent on Western trade. Instead, Yugoslavia at Tito's death found itself still faced with an enormous trade imbalance vis-à-vis the West and simultaneously increasingly dependent on the Soviet Union for oil and, ironically, concerned, in a world where power grows out of a barrel, that the Soviet Union would enjoy undue leverage.

Nothing succeeds like failure, however. Given the dual dependency, there was in practice little relationship between trade and politics. If we treat U.N. voting as a reasonable and readily quantifiable indication of foreign policy output, there was actually a negative correlation in Yugoslav voting alignment in the U.N. and change in Yugoslav trade patterns. Overall, similarly, no relationship can be detected in changes in Yugoslav trade and vot-

TABLE 2.3
Yugoslav Exports and Imports, 1957-1984

	% of Yugoslavia's Exports to			% of Yugoslavia's Imports from		
	Centrally Planned Economies	Developing Countries	Developed Market	Centrally Planned Economies	Developing Countries	Developed Market
1957	26.6	9.4	64.1	21.6	6.0	72.4
1958	29.0	16.4	54.6	28.7	11.5	59.8
1959	31.2	19.9	48.8	25.1	12.8	62.1
1960	32.4	19.4	48.2	25.8	16.7	57.5
1961	30.4	20.5	48.9	18.9	11.8	69.2
1962	24.4	22.8	52.8	21.9	10.5	67.5
1963	27.2	17.3	55.2	22.8	13.6	63.4
1964	35.2	15.3	49.5	29.3	13.7	57.0
1965	42.6	14.5	42.8	29.1	13.4	57.5
1966	37.3	14.1	48.6	32.2	11.4	56.3
1967	36.7	11.5	51.8	27.1	9.8	63.1
1968	35.1	12.6	52.3	28.6	8.5	62.9
1969	31.1	13.0	56.0	24.0	11.2	64.7
1970	30.8	10.7	58.6	20.7	10.2	68.9
1971	37.0	10.5	52.5	23.9	10.2	65.9
1972	36.1	7.3	56.6	24.8	10.0	65.3
1973	31.5	15.6	52.9	22.5	16.4	61.1
1974	35.8	19.3	44.8	21.2	19.7	59.2
1975	42.3	23.5	34.1	21.6	18.8	59.6
1976	38.1	22.4	39.6	25.8	20.2	54.0
1977	35.9	26.6	37.5	24.3	19.8	55.9
1978	38.2	26.8	35.1	24.3	20.1	55.6
1979	36.9	25.0	38.1	23.8	19.8	56.4
1980	41.1	24.3	34.5	27.1	21.0	51.9
1981	46.0	23.1	30.8	28.8	19.2	52.1
1982	46.9	26.4	26.7	31.7	19.0	49.3
1983	42.3	25.8	31.9	33.2	21.9	44.8
1984	42.2	23.3	34.5	29.2	27.5	43.3

SOURCE: International Monetary Fund, *Direction of Trade Statistics*, Annual.

ing shifts in the U.N. Pluralizing trade dependence very likely reduces leverage.

Closely related to trade patterns was a second attribute of Yugoslav nonalignment in the 1970s, namely the Yugoslav practice of using aid and credits from the external environment for internal developmental purposes. In this context, there is no need to detail the fluctuating pattern of Yugoslavia's external credits. (For the U.S. contribution, see U.S. Agency for International Development, 1961, 1973, 1978.) What is more interesting is that as the 1970s progressed, the Yugoslav leadership seems to have evolved a new economic strategy of independence. One central feature of Yugoslav nonalignment in the last years of Tito's life involved the realization that a viable strategy for internal economic development could involve increasing domestic political cohesion while, simultaneously, cultivating vigorously the economic penetration of the country by *plural* sources. Yugoslavia may in this respect be viewed as an organization engaged in a massive and impressively successful effort to extract grants from its external environment, just as local governments in the United States devote considerable energy and resources to playing the grant-getting game from various federal agencies, or as academic entrepreneurs attempt to finance a program of research, teaching, and service out of a plurality of grants from public funds and private foundation sources.

The academic-entrepreneur analogy is especially apt. The Yugoslavs were able to obtain funding for certain items on their developmental shopping list from several global "foundations" with institutional interests in particular dimensions of Yugoslav developmental aims, interests not often shared by some other external source of funds. The U.S.S.R. provided credits to build factories in Montenegro to produce goods to export to the U.S.S.R., a project the International Bank for Reconstruction and Development would be unlikely to finance, while the IBRD provided funds for, *inter alia*, cultivating the Adriatic and improving cattle raising on *private* farms in socialist Yugoslavia. Yugoslavia, in short, under Tito, learned the lesson Samuel P. Huntington claims for Thailand. "A government," Huntington wrote, "may [grant] access to private, government, and international transnational organizations in such a way as to further its own objectives. The widespread penetration of its society by transnational organizations will, obviously, have significant effects on society. . . . In the process [however], it may greatly strengthen itself as a government" [1973, pp. 364-365].

The third important component of nonalignment that was novel in the 1970s pertained to Yugoslav defense policies. One of the clearest costs of being unaligned, in the generic sense, is the burden of defense. During the nadir of Cominform-Yugoslav relations, expenditures for defense constituted one-sixth to one-fifth of Yugoslav national income. (It had been relatively high in the immediate post-World War II years as well.) More recently, defense expenditures have stabilized at between 4 percent to 6 percent of the gross material product (see Table 2.4). It is clear, nevertheless, that relatively speaking, Yugoslavia, like other nonbloc European states, expends a higher percentage of GNP on defense than do most of its counterparts in NATO or the WTO; these expenditures reflect the fact that with respect to security, Yugoslavia does not ever get a free ride while some of the aligned sometimes do.

More closely tied with the doctrine of nonalignment per se is the doctrine of general people's defense, based on reliance on one's own forces and premised, in the words of Nikola Ljubicic (former Defense Minister, and

TABLE 2.4
Yugoslav Defense Spending, 1952-1981 (As a percent of Gross Material Product)

Year	%	Year	%	Year	%	Year	%	Year	%
1952	19.3	1958	9.0	1964	5.4	1970	5.0	1976	5.6
1953	14.8	1959	8.0	1965	5.4	1971	4.9	1977	5.3
1954	12.6	1960	7.2	1966	5.1	1972	4.9	1978	4.8
1955	10.3	1961	7.4	1967	5.2	1973	4.7	1979	4.8
1956	9.9	1962	7.2	1968	5.7	1974	5.5	1980	5.0
1957	7.9	1963	6.2	1969	5.3	1975	5.7	1981	5.6*

SOURCE: 1952-1981, Stockholm International Peace Research Institute *Yearbooks*.
*The 1985 *Yearbook* provides a tentative figure for 1982 of 3.9 percent.

subsequently President of the Republic of Serbia), on the assumption that "In the event that a war is imposed, the whole of Yugoslavia would be a battlefield on which all of its nations and nationalities would jointly defend their freedom, independence, sovereignty and territorial integrity" [Ljubicic in Dimitrijevic, 1982, p. 10]. Treatments of the Yugoslav military and in particular the doctrine of general people's defense are legion [Jones, 1982; Dean, n.d.; Johnson, 1971]. In this context three points need to be stressed: 1).The official declaratory position is that Yugoslavia has "no preconceived idea of a particular or exclusive enemy" and that "the desire to change the essential character [of Yugoslavia] could derive from two basic reasons. . . . In Yugoslavia's self-managing socialism, some may find more disturbing the component suggested by the term 'self-managing,' and others may be alarmed by the term 'socialism' " [Dimitrijevic, 1982, pp. 6 and 8]. 2). There can be little doubt that the contemporary doctrine was formulated, in Dimitrijevic's slightly coy words, "approximately 15 years ago," i.e., after the Soviet invasion of Czechoslovakia. 3). There is a kind of interdependence among the three concepts, nonalignment, self-management, and general people's defense. The link in the case of nonalignment and general people's defense stems, obviously, from the notion of self-reliance. The link with regard to self-management and general people's defense relates to the decentralized nature of the political system and the national question. On this Dimitrijevic is quite explicit: "The internal logic of the system of self-management socialism requires that the armed forces should not be exempt from the process of socialization. If the process were to extend to all aspects of State authority . . . with the exception of the military sector . . . , this could have detrimental consequences, since the military would remain the only classical form of the State, from the hierarchical point of view, with foreseeable dangers of dominating other sectors and strengthening militarization" [1982, p. 8].

I have written thus far, with good reason, as though there were a consistency to Yugoslavia's alignment policies throughout the post-1949 and especially the post-1956 period. While appropriate, it is a perspective that warrants substantial qualification as it relates to Yugoslavia's ties with particular states. This is so partly because nonalignment as policy subsumes multiple orientations. It may be thought of as a policy space defining the limits of the policy debate wherein proponents of closer ties to the global west, east, and south advocate their respective positions. Moreover, not all relations with particular states, by any means, are to be understood by reference to Yugoslavia's nonalignment policy. Specific disputes, such as that concerning the treatment of Slavic minorities, have often driven relations with bordering states—e.g., Italy, Austria, and Bulgaria. Perhaps most importantly, the content of nonalignment has varied over time.

This is nicely illustrated by noting briefly the divergent state of Soviet-Yugoslav relations at various times after 1957—after, that is, it became clear that Yugoslavia was committed to a nonaligned, nonbloc policy. (The point could as easily be made by comparing the state of Yugoslav-Chinese relations at various junctures or American-Yugoslav relations. Who, for instance, in 1962 would ever have imagined that Tito would be the first foreign communist leader to lay a wreath at Mao's mausoleum?) Thus, the early 1960s were a period when Soviet-Yugoslav relations were particularly close, partly because of the onset of the Sino-Soviet conflict, partly because of the strongly anticolonialist thread of Yugoslav policy. Yugoslav behavior regarding East Germany and the Yugoslav response to Moscow's provocative resumption of nuclear tests in the middle of the 1961 Belgrade Conference of the Nonaligned prompted Western observers to worry if nonalignment meant nonalignment on the side of the Soviet Union.

In the early 1970s, too, there were grounds for believing that Yugoslavia was once again drawing closer to the Soviet Union. (The context, it will be recalled, included the U S. war in Vietnam, the renewed emphasis on Leninist themes—democratic centralism and cadre control most notably—pertaining to the structure of the Yugoslav League of Communists in the aftermath of the 1971 Croatian events, and the partial reorientation of Yugoslav trade away from Western Europe.) Tito himself gave cause for such speculation when in 1973 he declared that the Soviet invasion of Czechoslovakia—which Yugoslavia had vigorously condemned—"had been transcended" and that, contrary to the views of "some of our people in foreign affairs," "I do not think it is logical to equate the U.S.S.R. and the U.S. . . . [just] because both . . . are great powers" [*Vjesnik*, February 23, 1973]. Similarly, by participating with other communist states in showing solidarity with the Arab cause, Yugoslavia prompted some observers, including the then U.S. Ambassador to Yugoslavia, Laurence Silberman, to suspect Yugoslav nonalignment was pro-Soviet [1977].

By the end of the 1970s, on the other hand, Yugoslavia was increasingly

36

stressing the aspects of its foreign policy that differentiated it from Soviet foreign policy. Yugoslavia had made no major arms purchases from the U.S. since 1961. In 1976, it was actually announced that major U.S. arms sales to Yugoslavia were to be resumed, a decision that was relegated to the back burner at Yugoslav request later that same year. In October 1977, U.S. Secretary of Defense Harold Brown visited Yugoslavia; the Yugoslav Defense Minister General Ljubicic came to the United States in September 1978, and in May 1979 General Bernard Rogers, at that time U.S. Army Chief of Staff, visited with Yugoslav army commanders in Belgrade. Similarly, by the end of the 1970s, there existed a virtual military alliance between Yugoslavia and Romania, the target of which was obviously the Soviet Union [Zimmerman in Terry, ed., 1984]. Moreover, whereas in the 1960s Yugoslavia had been cast as one of the radicals within the nonaligned movement, by the end of the 1970s, it found itself defending the nonaligned against the claims of the contemporary "radicals" within the movement, headed by Cuba, Libya, and Vietnam, that the socialist camp and the nonaligned movement were natural allies against imperialism.

The year 1979, for instance, provided several dramatic occasions for Yugoslav actions that challenged Soviet interests. Throughout 1979, Yugoslavia and Cuba (the latter with strong Soviet encouragement) struggled over the themes to be stressed at the Sixth Conference of Nonaligned Nations that met in Havana in September. There were numerous indications that the Yugoslavs were bent on making certain that the nonaligned movement would be directed against both Western and Soviet interests in the Third World. One utterance that nicely captures the flavor of Yugoslavia's challenge to Soviet interests faulted Iraqi leaders for emphasizing "exclusively the anti-imperialist and anti-Zionist aims of the nonalignment movement" (U.S. and Israel) instead of taking a "like stand in the equally important direction of our struggle against hegemony and all forms of political and economic domination which are not classic imperalism" (the Soviet Union) [Radio Belgrade, February 6, 1979, in *Yearbook of International Communist Affairs*, 1980, p. 103]. Even more vivid testimony of the extent to which Yugoslavia had become ranged against Soviet interests, of course, was provided by the Yugoslav reactions to the Vietnamese invasion of Kampuchea and the Soviet invasion of Afghanistan, each of which suggested to Yugoslav elites that socialist states were less the natural ally of, and more a clear and present danger to, the nonaligned.

NONALIGNMENT: TRENDS IN THE 1980S

In 1980 Tito finally died. Although six years is a relatively brief time, we can, nevertheless, draw some tentative conclusions about future trends in Yugoslavia's alignment policy. The safest projection surely is that nonalignment will continue as the keystone of Yugoslav foreign policy. To have said this is not to say very much, but it is to say something: it excludes, for instance, membership in NATO, the WTO, Comecon, and probably the EEC. In the absence of intervention by the Soviet army, the complete breakup of the country, or the introduction of multiparty rule, nonalignment is highly attractive as a foreign policy umbrella covering the preferences of—and masking the divergences among—a heterogeneous coalition. Consequently, it strains credulity in a world in which the Soviet Union and the United States remain the major players to imagine circumstances in which nonalignment would be formally abandoned. Even in quite unlikely circumstances, nonalignment might well be retained. In a scenario, for instance, where the Soviet army props up a communist regime, such a leadership would very likely declare for "real" nonalignment—as did the Afghan regime after the Soviet invasion of Afghanistan.

The more likely domestic eventualities almost certainly imply the retention of a nonaligned foreign policy. Aside from a continuation of the status quo, there are three likely domestic alternatives: 1) A regime in which the Federation's power is enhanced vis-à-vis the republics' and is therefore more centralized, but in which there is a more thoroughgoing commitment to the market. (Such a regime could either be more or less repressive than the current one.) 2) A "strong-hand" regime with a strong—Serbian—unitarist strand. (Such a regime might look like Romania or Jaruzelski's Poland. In either case, the military would play a central role.) 3) A regime in which Muslim influence, mostly from Bosnia-Hercegovina, would be greatly enhanced, probably at the expense, largely, of the Slovenes. (Such a regime would be more akin to traditionalist Leninist systems than is the present one.)

For none of these scenarios does it seem likely that there would be much incentive to abandon nonalignment. At the same time, however, the content of nonalignment would almost certainly change. Thus, a more heavily Muslim role in the coalition might produce a greater attachment to the global south and to anti-American, anticolonial policies; a more market-oriented, albeit less federated, Yugoslavia might be more pro-Western; and a military-dominated firm-hand system might be somewhat more pro-Soviet, but such tendencies are far more likely within the nonalignment rubric than outside it.

Glimmers of these possibilities are already visible. There have been recent attacks on Muslim resurgence and a concomitant interest in greater links to the Arab world. Hamdija Pozderac, President of the Bosnia-Hercegovina Central Committee, has attacked intellectuals and the clergy for Pan-Islamic sentiments. According to Vojislav Seselj, "Some members of the Central Committee of the League of Communists of Bosnia-Hercegovina and some groups in the Central Committee are flirting'' with them as well [*Delo*, December 25, 1982, in *Borba*, January 18, 1983, and translated by *FBIS*, January 27, 1983, p. I 10]. *NIN* [January 16, 1983] summarizes the same article and mentions—as does *Borba*—Seselj's criticisms of the members of the Sarajevo Faculty of Political Science for their statements about Khaddafi's Green Book. Between 1982 and 1984, there was increasingly open resistance by persons in the Croatian republic party leadership to pro-Western centralizers, i.e., to those who would reduce the power of the republic party organizations and cooperate actively with the International Monetary Fund. During this same period, jokes that implied a possible military takeover—''How far is Yugoslavia from Poland?'' ''About a year''— were ubiquitous in Yugoslavia. More portentous surely, and probably more significant, was Mitja Ribicic's recent pointed reminiscence about Tito's handling of the first strikes in Trbovlje, Slovenia. ''Tito at that time advocated an ideopolitical approach, in contrast to Rankovic, who was in favor of administrative police methods. With Tito's approach, the causes of the strikes were removed. Had some kind of—if I may say so—'Polish manner' of resolving this incident been used then, it would have been decisive and very difficult for Yugoslavia, not merely for Slovenia. Tito would never have allowed it'' [*Politika*, May 25, 1983, in *FBIS*, June 7, 1983, p. I 27].

Moreover, it remains the case that the possibility of some domestic scenarios is constrained by the widely perceived desirability of being able to claim that Yugoslavia is different from the countries of Soviet-style socialism and from the Western ''bourgeois'' democracies. Hence there remains a link between loose bipolarity, nonalignment, and the likely continuation of self-managing socialism.

My suspicion, however, is that such a link is a bit more tenuous than it was circa 1950 when the core elements of self-management were introduced. Whereas self-management was initially a function of nonalignment, it is likely that in the policy-relevant future the changing content of nonalignment will depend in considerable measure on the changing content of self-management. Moreover, second-generation leaders are generally less ideologically driven than their predecessors. It may well not matter as much as it did to Tito, Kardelj, and Bakaric whether the system is seen as being distinctive from that of one or the other superpowers. Tito's heirs may aspire to achieve legitimacy domestically by other means—although in the mid 1980s it was still a standard polemical ploy to discredit someone by labeling his or her views as bourgeois, anarcho-liberal, or Cominformist.

Should the emphasis on distinctiveness be reduced, this would link with other ways the post-Titoist leadership may define nonalignment differently than did Tito. These would be commensurate with the pattern of other second-generation postrevolutionary leaderships—the Sadats, as opposed to

39

their revolutionary fathers, the Nassers. Generally, second-generation leaders tend to attach greater significance to tangible goals of domestic development and are less concerned with global symbolism and status. Something like that seems to be happening in Yugoslavia where there have been some changes in the content of nonalignment and evidence of undercurrents that suggest some rather tough thinking about the rationale for nonalignment.

There is some evidence that Yugoslavia's policy has become somewhat less global in domain. Ronald Linden's findings on Yugoslav interactions with other states in 1975-1976 and in 1980-1981 suggest that with Tito's death there has been an increased orientation regionally toward Europe and the Middle East [1982, Table v]. The fact that in the immediate post-Tito years, budgetary concerns have prompted the closing of several Yugoslav missions in the Third World also speaks volumes. (Note, for instance, Dolanc's comment that "1353 missions abroad" is "a striking figure. Of course there is a question of the rationality or efficiency of these" [*Tanjug* in *FBIS*, October 5, 1982, p. I 11].) Given Tito's globalist bent and the symbolic and charismatic gains he derived from nonalignment, it is difficult to imagine him either closing the missions or basing such a decision on cost considerations. A distinguished Yugoslav economist told me in January 1983 that he was going to propose a project to undertake a cost-benefit analysis of nonalignment to ascertain whether and exactly to what extent Yugoslavia's policies in the Third World have been beneficial. Whether such a project ever transpires, it bespeaks a way of approaching nonalignment that simply was not considered appropriate in the Tito era.

It does not imply that the Yugoslav leadership is likely to conclude that there is a reason to abandon nonalignment on pragmatic grounds. Rather it is to stress that the argument for nonalignment is now one based on its efficaciousness. In the words of the editor of the major Yugoslav international journal *Review of International Affairs*, "If we were to make a comparative survey of what the great bloc powers and the nonaligned countries have achieved in realizing their strategic aims in the period following the Second World War, we would see that it was precisely the bloc powers that were— and have remained—the synonym of inefficiency, while the nonaligned countries were the synonym of effectiveness in international relations" [Petkovic, 1983, p. 9]. Similarly, there is every reason to suspect that the Yugoslav leadership will continue to regard the attachment to global symbols and institutions—as opposed to a globalist policy—as instrumentally justifiable. For a small state like Yugoslavia, the commitment to universal symbols and institutions will remain; Yugoslavia is convinced that a broadly based nonalignment movement "is the best means of protecting its own interests and also serves the interests of the world" [Dimitrijevic,

1982, p. 11]. Any independent communist Yugoslavia will be vociferous in its condemnation of efforts anywhere to overturn a regime or to alter the borders of any nonaligned socialist state—whether it be in Asia, Africa, or Latin America.

Likewise, continuity is the most plausible prognosis for the notion that an important component of nonalignment involves being penetrated economically by plural sources as a way of safeguarding and improving the state's capacity for mobilization. Even—or perhaps especially—in hard economic times the post-Tito leadership is aware that it can strengthen itself as a government by negotiating credits simultaneously with the West and the Soviet Union.

What a more pragmatic calculus about nonalignment may affect is the general Yugoslav orientation toward the global south. The modest turn toward more regional and less grandiose policy may be a harbinger. A nonalignment policy that is less based on symbolic goods and more grounded on tangible benefits could be more shaped by those (in Slovenia for instance) who have said "our place is in Europe." Certainly between 1982 and 1985 the commitment with respect to trade orientation has been directed toward greater trade proportionally with Europe, though, politics absolutely aside, the proclivity for trade with Europe will be constrained by the knowledge that economically Yugoslavia has ample reasons—its energy deficiency most notably—for close links with the Soviet Union and the Middle East.

Therefore, if we were to assess the prospects for Yugoslavia's nonalignment policy over the near term, at least in the absence of fundamental changes in the regime, we would expect a more regionally oriented policy than heretofore, one based more on an awareness of the benefits that can accrue from occupying a strategic position between the two blocs and less on an assumption that it is important to mark off Yugoslavia doctrinally from the superpowers. As for relations with particular states, there the actions of others become equally determinative and the outcome far less subject to extrapolation. What is likely to continue, however, is the Yugoslav leadership's use of the international environment as a resource for addressing internal developmental goals and the ritualized deference to nonalignment, whatever its variable content, as the one foreign policy symbol with which the multinational coalition can identify.

3

INTERNATIONAL-NATIONAL LINKAGES
AND THE GAME OF POLITICS
IN YUGOSLAVIA

Chapter 2 argued that self-management, however variable its content, had been initially adopted largely as a way of distancing Yugoslavia ideologically from the superpowers. This chapter examines the links between the international environment and the game of politics in "self-managing" Yugoslavia. Our concern here is twofold. One concern is the evolution of the Yugoslav elite's political and organizational strategy for assuring national cohesion in a world of states and, one hastens to emphasize, in an ethnically pluralistic society [LaPalombara, 1975, pp. 305-332; Burg, 1983]. The other is the way events in the international environment, or which are perceived to have direct links to the international environment, influence Yugoslav policy processes and thus the resource allocation dimension of "system security."

The two are parallel and interrelated phenomena. Out of the evolving strategy for achieving national cohesion has emerged the institutional setting in which the game of politics is played. These institutions can, and in the Yugoslav context have been intended to, shape and influence the operation of political processes. Likewise the experience in concrete cases with particular patterns of behavior has clearly provided the context in which changes in strategy and institutions occurred.

What follows therefore is a description first of the evolving Yugoslav strategy of political organization. This is followed by a description of a paradigm for analyzing Yugoslav policy processes illustrated by several relevant episodes from the Tito and post-Tito eras. All the cases emphasize that in analyzing the political evolution of Yugoslavia, international-national linkages are ignored only at great cost. At the same time, the paradigm is intended to provide the reader with an approach that is generally relevant to an understanding of Yugoslav "domestic" politics whether or not the particular event involves a major international-national linkage. The concluding section of the chapter addresses the implication of several policy issues involving international-national linkages in the post-Tito era for the evolution of Yugoslav political institutions in the early 1980s.

The Leninist and Titoist "Models"

To comprehend Yugoslav nonalignment requires an understanding of Yugoslav ties with the U.S.S.R. before the Stalin-Tito break. To comprehend how the Yugoslav communists succeeded in seizing power and how they managed to withstand Stalin's attack in 1948 necessitates an understanding of Yugoslav political and organizational structures at the time of power seizure and in 1948. After World War II, Yugoslavia was a little Soviet Union that set out with a vengeance to imitate the Motherland of Socialism. The Yugoslavs largely emulated the Soviet pattern of coming to power. There were differences, to be sure; in many respects the best analogue is with the communist seizure of power in China, rather than in Russia. The Yugoslav communists relied much more heavily on the peasants than did the Bolsheviks, and the fundamental transformation of Yugoslav society and the building of local political institutions were already well launched by the end of World War II. The Bolsheviks, by contrast, seized central political power and proceeded subsequently to transform the society and institutionalize the revolution outside the major urban areas. Nevertheless, like the Bolsheviks, the Yugoslavs came to power more or less on their own; they created a monolithic party organization headed by a charismatic leader; and they set out immediately to transform Yugoslav society through such characteristically Soviet means as nationalization and expropriation. Not only did they emulate the Soviet political model in seizing power and organizing the state and party apparatus, the Yugoslavs in the 1940s patterned their economy after the Soviet Union: a command economy, forced savings, and deferred gratification, five-year plans, full employment, state foreign trade monopoly, bilateral trade flows, and autarky.

The Leninist model also served Tito in good stead during his clash with Stalin in 1948. When the Soviet Union attempted to impose satellite status on Yugoslavia through the use of such traditional control mechanisms as joint stock companies, and the appointment of Soviet advisers at strategic points in the governmental apparatus and in the economy, these efforts came to nought, largely because Yugoslavia had emulated the Soviet pattern. Having paralleled the Soviet Union by building socialism in one country, a little Soviet Union would not easily become a satellite of the real one.

After the Cominform-Yugoslav clash, a re-evaluation of the Leninist model of political organization took place. In the 1950s and 1960s, the assumption, grounded in the experience of World War II and the Cominform clash, that the institutionalized Leninist party is the most effective organizational strategy for resisting external influence was gradually and fitfully called into question. Beginning in the early 1950s with the attention to

43

workers' self-management and a decision to relabel the party a league of communists, Tito and the other members of the Yugoslav leadership began to stress the extent to which the party itself and the relations between the LCY and the society diverged from the patterns associated with a "traditional ruling party" and "state socialism." Slowly, a more conciliatory and consensual strategy evolved with respect to regime-society relations.

The defining characteristic of that strategy was that the surest method for maintaining national cohesion was a posture of confidence in the Yugoslav citizenry by the elite. The regime's involvement in society became markedly less intrusive. The goal of collectivization was, for all intents and purposes, abandoned. Precensorship was abandoned and controls over the press reduced sizably. Workers' self-management symbolized the commitment to participatory forms of industrial control; toleration of strikes bespoke a tolerance for spontaneous interest articulation not associated with traditional Leninist systems. The gradual acceptance of market socialism in the 1960s connoted a conscious decision to devolve decisional competence from the political system to the market. Genuine devolution of power and authority away from the central party leadership was also evident in the movement toward an authentically federal system and in investing formal state institutions with functions associated with such institutions in Western institutional systems. Finally, any list of policy shifts away from the regime-society relations characteristic of Leninist party systems should include the decision taken in early 1960s to open the borders, thus allowing the outmigration of Yugoslav workers, primarily to Western Europe, a phenomenon which, as we shall see in Chapter 4, took on immense proportions by the early 1970s.

Many departures from the Leninist model were also implemented with respect to the party itself and the party's relationship to "sociopolitical organizations" such as the Socialist Alliance, the trade unions, and the state per se. To be sure, Milovan Djilas' efforts in the mid-1950s to democratize the LCY proved abortive. (Djilas, it will be recalled, came to advocate both the democratization of the LCY and a competitive party system.) However, after the 1966 ouster of secret police head Aleksandar Rankovic, the pace of the departure from the Leninist model accelerated. Rankovic's ouster was followed by a series of institutional changes designed to provide a context in which economic reform and political decentralization could flourish.

In addition to harnessing the police to the party, more fundamental institutional changes were accomplished. The institutional configuration of the party at the federal level was altered, as was the relation of the Yugoslav League of Communists to the republics' parties. After bloody riots in Kosovo (which had been a virtual Rankovic fiefdom) in 1968, both Kosovo and Vojvodina were given the status of Socialist Autonomous Provinces and the right to use their native languages (Albanian and Hungarian) in public institutions; and each began to take on many of the functions and connections to the center one associates with republic status, even though each remained a constituent part of the Republic of Serbia [Burg, 1983, p. 74].

Certain changes in the relationship of the party to the government, the enterprises, and to such "sociopolitical organizations" as the Socialist Alliance and the trade unions also were effected. At the center, the previously superordinate role of the Executive Committee (Politburo) was restricted and a broad-gauge Presidium of the Central Committee established. Democratic centralism was defined more loosely than before. Similarly, the powers of the republic party organizations were enhanced vis-à-vis those of the LCY, a development commensurate with the genuine decentralization of governmental competence to the republics and provinces. In words reminiscent of Milovan Djilas in 1954, it was insisted 1) that the League's chief area of activity should be that "of ideology and ideological-political struggle" because the party "has not yet completely freed itself from the practical matters, especially economic, and also from all state functions"; 2) that there should be a strict separation between the party and either the state or the economy; and 3) that communists should act in governmental bodies "as members of these bodies," not as instructed representatives of trade unions, the Socialist Alliance, or the LCY [Mijalko Todorovic in *Politika*, April 30, May 1, 2, 1966, in RFE *Research*, May 5, 1966, p. 1]. At the same time, increasingly important and autonomous roles were to be allotted to the trade unions and the Socialist Alliance. These roles accorded with the view that the single party system should gradually atrophy, giving way ultimately to a no-party system. With the LCY confined to an ideological role, with power increasingly decentralized to republic organs, with the competence of the trade unions and the Socialist Alliance enlarged, the party would begin to wither away.

Perhaps the culmination of the institutional developments that followed Rankovic's ouster and oriented the system in a more decentralized and depoliticized direction, however, came with Tito's decision in September 1970 to establish the State Presidency. Indeed, the conception of the State Presidency smacked of a confederative scheme; "the best people from individual republics" (three from each republic and two apiece from the autonomous provinces of Kosovo and Vojvodina) would join Tito, the President of the Republic, in a broad forum, in order—in the words of Edvard Kardelj, "to make individual republics not feel as if, so to say, they are provinces of a big state, but rather as subjects [who] realize their functions through such a body" [as quoted in RFE *Research*, February 3, 1970, p. 7]. After Tito's death, according to the official line, these same "best people" would rotate the presidency on a yearly basis. The automatic nature of the rotation would symbolize the nationality-based, consensual character of Yugoslav politics.

THE RETURN TO LENINIST SYMBOLS

Hopes for a consensually based confederative Yugoslavia held together at the top after Tito's death by an assemblage of the "best people" sharing a common attachment to self-management and nonalignment were severely shaken by the events in Croatia in 1971. (It will be recalled that these events prompted an offer from Brezhnev for assistance.) These events set into motion much the same kind of soul searching as the Rankovic ouster and resulted ultimately in an equally substantial institutional transformation. During the year following the Zagreb strike, the Yugoslav citizenry witnessed an intense and articulate dispute about the proper organization of Yugoslav society. One side—advocates of what might be called the Austrian variant—demanded that the process of democratization be intensified, and expressed an almost social democratic definition of mass-leadership relations. The other side gave vent to a much more typically Leninist conception of intraparty, party-state, and regime-societal norms; they might be termed proponents of the Romanian orientation. What was at stake was nothing less than the basic orientation of Yugoslav domestic and foreign policy and the general configuration of the Yugoslav political system. As Marko Nikezic—former Foreign Minister and in 1971-1972 president of the Serbian party—remarked, what was at issue was "not only a confrontation of different interests and methods, but a confrontation of different, broader concepts of problems of the socialist society" [*FBIS*, December 8, 1971, p. I 3].

To Nikezic—the most prominent advocate of extending democratization—the Croatian developments signified, as he declared in 1971, "The importance of freeing ourselves from our own Communist conservatism which, being unable to respond to the changed needs of society would try to master the difficulties of the present stage by returning to the old norms and relations, to a renewal of ideology and a renewal of the party and so forth." The events in Zagreb revealed, furthermore, "the consequences of a long-lasting monopoly of the top party and state leadership," and the dangers of "monolithic unity, that is, a total concentration of power at all levels." The remedy for past mistakes, he observed, can in the future only be overcome by a "united policy," which Nikezic, consistent with his overall consensual perspective, defined as "one approved by the masses of the people": "If there is no such policy," he continued, "no leadership, under our conditions and system, could stand, that is, would actually withstand the destructive effect of the absence of a democratically determined united policy'' [*FBIS*, December 8, 1971, pp. I 4-I 5].

Ten months later, in September 1972, Nikezic took his case once more to the press, granting an interview, significantly entitled "Democratization— Condition of Unity," to the Ljubljana newspaper *Delo*, which was reproduced in the Belgrade weekly *NIN* [September 10, 1972, pp. 34-37]. There he reaffirmed his previous stand. He called for the development of a "mass movement which will struggle for the interests of the working class and the young generation," and he urged the strengthening of the role of the trade unions. He attacked the tendency in the party to view issues in narrow cadre terms: "As soon as we begin to discuss matters as strictly organizational or cadre problems, as party problems in the narrow sense of the term, we fall into . . . error." He called repeatedly for greater democratization in the formation of policy, both on the federal level and in the republics. "Democratization," he reiterated, "in the formation of policy is the condition of unity," and added, "One should have no illusions that six or eight autocracies would create a federation of equal rights. Very quickly that would result, legally, in a single bureaucratic center."

In sharp contrast to Nikezic's position was that of Tito and, by the fall 1972 at least, Stane Dolanc. Dolanc may initially have opposed the recentralizing thrusts. An important study published in Belgrade in 1978 by Dragan Markovic and Savo Krzavac, *Liberalizam od Djilasa do danas [Liberalism from Djilas to Today]*, states that at a meeting between Tito and Nikezic in December 1971, in the immediate aftermath of the Croatian events, Dolanc took part and "spoke about the enemy acts which emanate from positions of bureaucratic *etatism*, neo-Cominformism, unitarism, and centralism" [Markovic and Krzavac, 1978, p. 121]. In any event, by the fall of 1972 Dolanc was playing an important role in implementing Tito's shift to a more unitarian and Leninist posture. For Tito and Dolanc in the fall of 1972, the lessons of the Zagreb strike were dramatically opposed to those derived by Nikezic. For Nikezic, the need was for a policy approved by the masses and democratization; for Tito and Dolanc, the main danger was liberalism. Their policy prescriptions were those typically associated with the Leninist tradition. Democratic centralism must be observed: "We have forgotten that . . . ," Tito declared, and that fact is "one of the basic causes of the situation in our country." In the words of the September 18, 1972, "Letter" by Tito and the LCY Executive Bureau: "There has been a fair amount of wavering, inconsistency, and deviation from the principle of democratic centralism." Moreover, "Cadre policy has also been neglected," Tito said. As the "Letter" (I follow the Yugoslav practice by capitalizing it) declares, "The League of Communists must consolidate its role and influence in the field of cadre policy . . . . Responsibility for constructive social and state affairs [must] be entrusted to people who will perform these duties in the interest of the working class and the development of socialist self-management.'' To ensure such an occurrence, the party, in the words of the ''Letter,'' must be ''transformed into the kind of organization of revolutionary action that is capable of translating its stands and policy into life more efficiently.'' ''We have never believed,'' Tito declared, ''that organized democratic institutions in the state and society represent separation or disassociation of the League of Communists from the obligations and the responsibility to act as an ideopolitical force in an organized manner; Communists in all institutions should implement the LCY Policy'' [*Tanjug* in *FBIS*, October 18, 1972, pp. I 3-12]. Finally, opportunism must be fought: ''The toleration of views and political conduct that are at variance with the ideology and policy of the League of Communists'' must be terminated.

It may have been a foregone conclusion that, in the end, Tito's position would prevail. Nevertheless, Nikezic's view was scarcely an isolated one. He had strong support in Slovenia and probably in Macedonia. In Serbia (including Vojvodina) Nikezic's position was heartily endorsed. Tito himself commented in his concluding speech to an assemblage of the *aktiv* of Serbia convened in October 1972 that ''When it came to the point that people should critically refer to the shortcomings which I briefly dealt with in my introductory speech, I noticed in the very beginning that the discussion took a much different orientation than I wanted.'' It is certain that Tito never commanded a majority at the meeting of the Serbian *aktiv*. In discussing that session, he noted (in words reminiscent of Nikita Khrushchev's ''arithmetic majority'') that, ''when a discussion is held concerning party policy, its results, and shortcomings, the number of speakers for or against a certain thesis and [their] assessment of a situation—[are] not [decisive factors] when it comes to revolutionary choice and assessment, especially when this occurs in a forum, because life bypasses forums'' [*FBIS*, October 18, 1972, p. I 12].

In the end, of course, Tito did carry the day. The upshot of the polemic was Nikezic's resignation and in the short run the resounding resumption of utterances demanding a return to Leninist institutions, a victory which seemed to imply that Tito had cast his lot with the Leninist party as the surest institutional strategy for maintaining national integration after his death [Zimmerman, 1976; Rusinow, 1977]. It was a decision that seemed to imply profound consequences for Yugoslav political institutions.

And indeed, in the years immediately after the ''Letter,'' democratic centralism was made more confining for dissenting party members at given levels and some recentralization of competence at the center at the expense of republic party organizations took place. There was no more talk in the early 1970s of the withering away of the party; the notion that there should be a rigid separation between party and state was also abandoned; and party control over the mass media was reestablished.

Nowhere, perhaps, was the apparent return to traditional Leninist organizational forms more evident than in the evolution of thinking about the institution of the State Presidency. As initially conceived in 1970, it evoked an almost confederative air: the "best people" from individual republics would, after Tito's death, rotate the presidency on a yearly basis, thus symbolizing the nationality-based consensual character of Yugoslav politics. More recently, it has appeared that the State Presidency would be made up of prominent party figures of very long standing, one from each republic and the president of the League of Communists. In 1978, however, those persons—other than the president of the LCY—being considered for appointment to the State Presidency were no longer ones of great stature, but, in Slobodan Stankovic's words, people "belonging to the second, if not the third, rank of the country's leadership" [RFE *Research*, April 7, 1978, p. 5]. In the LCY, the Presidium was strengthened and was made up of real heavyweights. The implication seemed straightforward: the intention was to return to a conception in which the pre-eminent political organization was something approximating a party politburo; the State Presidency as a collective leadership had been downgraded. With respect to political organization, therefore, the case could be made in the early 1970s that the Yugoslavs had returned in the 1970s to their 1948 strategy: back to the Partisans who had stood together in the war and back to the Leninist party structures which had served Tito so well in his confrontation with Stalin. In the 1970s the "organizational weapon" had been reinvoked, and, in actuality, with some success. By purging the republic party leaderships and reasserting party domination over the mass media, Yugoslav leaders created conditions that were far less propitious than those in 1970-1971 for opposing the central party leadership. Tito was not just engaging in New Year's Eve hyperbole when he declared at the onset of 1977 that "I want to stress again that the unity of our working people has never been greater than today" [*Politika*, December 31, 1976, January 1, 2, 1977]. He had made it more difficult than in 1970-1971 for potential counterelites either to utilize republic party organizations as a power base or to mobilize the masses against the central leadership.

Consensus and Authoritarianism

Writing in the 1980s, with the clarity that hindsight provides, it seems that the changes were less profound than the reinvocation of such symbols as Lenin, democratic centralism, and dictatorship of the proletariat implied. While it was correct to say that the LCY Presidium had been strengthened

49

and had become something akin to a politburo, it was a governing committee of 24, not a dozen. The Presidium included three members from each republic, two from the provinces, and one from the military party organization, plus Tito as president of the LCY. Significantly, the even smaller Executive Committee (before that the Executive Bureau) was eliminated at the eleventh LCY Congress in 1978.

Moreover, the republic party organizations retained many significant powers vis-à-vis the center. Tito had "established the right of central organs independently to determine their own internal organization and operation, to expel individuals from their ranks, and to remove regional leaders from office." He "did not establish the right of central organs independently to appoint either their own members or the leaders of regional organizations." [Burg, 1983, p. 186]. Nor was the practice of consensual decisionmaking abandoned; rather, the notion of "harmonization" of positions continued the norm in the party (and in the government).

If, furthermore, we examine the notion of democratic centralism as it evolved during the 1970s, we find that its content shifted rather substantially. The same Stane Dolanc who in 1972 had defended democratic centralism in its traditional Leninist sense, in December 1976 attacked those who "believe that in the name of democratic centralism or in the name of some would-be unity, they can realize their interests primarily with the help of the League of Communists' authority" [*Tanjug* in *FBIS*, December 30, 1976, p. I 14]. At the Eleventh LCY Congress in 1978, a major effort to increase the democratic dimensions of democratic centralism was written into the party statutes. In the new formulation, "LCY members whose views . . . have minority support may retain their own stands on these issues but are obligated to accept and implement the decisions adopted by the majority. Any activity that [impedes implementation of] decisions adopted would represent a type of group-forming and factional activity." As a March 1978 *Tanjug* report stated, "According to the [previously existing] policy, a League of Communists' member [did] not have the right to retain his views" when in the minority [*FBIS*, March 23, 1978, p. I 8].

Likewise, the subsection on democratic centralism in the LCY statutes legitimates the center's interference in local party organizations as well as in nonparty organizations, and characterizes the central organs as "the unified political leadership of the entire" LCY. Nevertheless, the republican, provincial, and military party organizations continue to choose members of the central organs and are allotted, according to the LCY statute, "equal responsibility" "for the construction and execution of the unified policy of the League" [Burg, 1983, p. 315]. In practice, furthermore, it was quite clear that decisions would be taken consensually and that the binding will of the center over the republics and provinces would occur only if the republic leaders chose to be bound. As Pozderac expressed it a year after Tito's death, "the highest form of democratic centralism is the unanimity of a decision." [*NIN*, July 19, 1981, in Burg, 1983, p. 349]. This novel notion of democratic centralism nicely captures the power relations between center and republics absent the integrating force of Tito.

Despite the purges of the Croatian party leadership in 1971 and the Serbian leadership in 1972, it now appears that in many respects the republican party organs were actually strengthened during the 1970s. As we have just seen, there was no fundamental redistribution of power in favor of the central party organization at the expense of the republic organs. Moreover, the attack on the market and on "technocratism" redistributed power away from the enterprise managers, the workers' self-management units, and the economy to the regional party organizations and the political system. As Dusan Bilandzic observed in 1981, "During the past decade, the most powerful influence on social development has been the republic political administrative centers" [*Nase teme*, 1981, p. 1866]. Communal and regional party leaders have greatly broadened the domain of their power so that with Tito, and especially in his absence, the re-Leninization of the party turned out to be much more a phenomenon observable at the republic and local levels than at the level of the Federation. At the center, consensus and harmonization among the six or eight—and that was a key ambiguity—regional organs remained the key words, a blend that can best be characterized as consociational authoritarianism (see also Lenard Cohen in Vucinich, ed., 1982). (Ian Lustick [1979, pp. 325-344 at p. 328] aptly characterizes consociationalism as referring to "an image of an elite cartel [in a divided society] whose members share an overarching commitment to the survival of the arena within which their groups compete "and enforce, within their groups, the terms of mutually acceptable compromises." Lustick regards consociationalism as a concept applicable to all societies, not—as is traditionally the case in the literature—as a form of democracy.)

With regard to the government, also, the principles of harmonization and consensus prevailed. Parity became the watchword in cadre matters and elsewhere, and the change from a twenty-three-member to a nine-member State Presidency in 1974 altered, in this respect, the near-parity status of the autonomous provinces to one of complete equality with the republics. The overt commitment to increase the role of the LCY notwithstanding, the role of the governmental Federal Executive Council (FEC) was also actually strengthened in the 1970s. The 1974 Constitution provided in Article 362 that in the execution of policy the FEC "May not receive directives or orders from . . . other sociopolitical communities, nor may they follow such directives and/or orders" [*Constitution*, 1974, p. 279]. Moreover, the FEC is the central institution mandated to govern in the absence of consensus.

Article 301 authorizes the FEC to adopt temporary measures if "it is indispensable to prevent or eliminate major disruptions on the market, or that the nonsettlement of these questions might result in serious harm for the social community, might endanger national defense interests, or might result in unequal economic relations between the Republics and the Autonomous Provinces, or if this would render impossible the fulfilment of obligations towards insufficiently developed Republics and Autonomous Provinces, or the fulfilment of [Yugoslavia's] commitments [to] other countries and international organizations" [p. 248; also Mujacic, *Politicka misao*, 1978, pp. 548-552; Burg, 1983].

Temporary measures adopted under Article 301 are valid for a year and may be renewed for another year. Article 302 of the 1974 Constitution in turn provides that "if a bill on temporary measures has not been passed in the Chamber of Republics and Provinces by a two-thirds majority vote of all delegates to the Chamber, the SFRY Presidency may proclaim that this bill, in the text adopted by the majority of all delegates to the Chamber, be applied pending final passage of the bill. . . ." [p. 249; also Burg, 1983; Mujacic, *Politicka misao*, 1978].

Thus Tito's reinvocation of Leninist symbols at the beginning of the 1970s re-established the minimal social and political consensus requisite for governing. The dominant institutions of Yugoslav politics, however, continued throughout the decade to be a blend of central and republic, and increasingly provincial, party organs and governmental organs. These were institutions that recognized and legitimated elite pluralism—"the pluralism of self-managing interests" in Kardelj's words [1978]—while discouraging and indeed deterring mass participation, participation that would, it was feared, exacerbate the pluralistic cleavages in Yugoslav society and threaten intervention from without.

THE GAME OF POLITICS IN YUGOSLAVIA: A POLICY PARADIGM

In such an institutional setting, there were ample opportunities for the vigorous articulation of interests, and manifest evidence of the way the game of politics is played in Yugoslavia. The paradigm used in the remainder of this chapter to depict those politics is based on two seminal articles by Theodore Lowi [1964, 1967] which substantiated the link between issue area and policy process in American politics. What I have done elsewhere [1973] is to argue that Lowi's insights into American domestic and foreign policy processes can be combined and extended to reasonably integrated modern states that have nontotalitarian, but not necessarily democratic, institutions. As the previous section suggests, Yugoslavia is such a state.

Lowi's two articles dealt with American domestic politics and American

foreign policy respectively. In those articles he identified a total of four issue areas ("arenas of power" in Lowi's terms) where divergent policy processes may be observed. Each issue area is characterized by different actors,
different patterns of interaction and a different power structure; I have argued it is possible to identify two questions, the answers to which serve as
the criteria for categorizing a specific policy, and which when answered,
should permit specification of the nature of the actors and the patterns of
interaction. The questions are: 1) Is a decision perceived to be symmetrical
in its impact on politically relevant domestic political actors? 2) Are the political goods in question exclusively tangible? The paradigm and the characteristics are summarized in Table 3.1.

The arena of distribution (arena I) is, in this scheme, one where the impact on the domestic society is symmetrical and the political goods are exclusively tangible. These goods are also highly subject to disaggregation
and are best exemplified by what in American politics have been called pork
barrel items. Individuals and firms are the actors in the political game: since
the political goods are readily subject to being parceled out, nearly everyone

TABLE 3.1
Issue Areas and Policy Processes: A Summary

| | | *Domestic impact symmetrical?* | |
		YES	NO

Political goods exclusively tangible?	YES	I. *Distribution*
		
		Primary political actors
		  individual, firm
		Patterns of interaction
		  logrolling; "unprincipled"
		  alliances of uncommon interests
		Power structure
		  nonconflicting elite with
		  support groups
			II. *Regulation*
			
			Primary Political actors
			  group
			Patterns of interaction
			  "the coalition"; shared subject
			  matter interest aggregation
			Power structure
			  pluralist, multicentered

	NO	III. *Protection/Interaction*
		
		Primary political actors
		  individuals "without their
		  institutions"
		Patterns of interaction
		  "team norms"
		Power structure
		  highly elitist
			IV. *Redistribution*
			
			Primary political actors
			  classes, movements,
			  generations
			Patterns of interaction
			  "peak associations"
			Power structure
			  conflictual elite:
			  elite and counterelite

		CONSENSUAL	CONFLICTUAL
		Type of politics	

53

(read: everyone who counts politically) gets his share. (The current argot "a piece of the action" captures this notion nicely.) Logrolling constitutes the name of the game. Typically, "unprincipled" alliances of uncommon interests are constructed. Needless to add, such politics are relatively consensual, taking place within a largely nonconflicting elite.

Lowi's arena of regulation (arena II) has groups as its primary actors. In this arena, the patterns of interaction involve groups of the like-minded. Who gets what is decided as a result of the fact that the goods, while tangible, are not as subject to disaggregation as they are in distributive politics and their impact on domestic society is asymmetrical. Conflict consequently is greater. Where it is often difficult in the distributive arena to identify specific losers, there are always losers in regulative politics. In the short run, the regulatory decision involves a direct choice as to who will be indulged and who deprived. Some will not obtain a liquor license in Ann Arbor, just as some will not obtain an overseas air route.

The third arena identified is the one that is traditionally most associated with foreign policy. For twentieth-century multipurpose states it is in fact merely one issue area largely devoted to foreign policy—what I have called the protective and interactive arena. The actors are individuals, though largely those individuals, as Lowi puts it, stripped of their institutions, who have a highly legitimate, role-engendered claim to participation in the policy process. Hence, the power structure is highly elitist. Team norms prevail as decisions are made which, it is perceived, are such that the impact of the decision will be symmetrical for all citizens of the state: in a crisis (protection) the external event or actor is thought to be uniformly threatening; in noncrisis circumstances, no internal resources are involved, and there are no short-run political consequences. (Students of world politics will recognize the borrowing from Arnold Wolfers' [1962, pp. 15-16] famous pole of power and pole of indifference.) Occurrences of the latter type are obviously likely to be rare. When they do occur, they will occur most often when states are attempting to facilitate the exchange of information and diplomats, to regularize the international exchange of mail, or otherwise enhance state interaction. Like distributive politics, the politics of protection and interaction are more consensual than conflictual. Unlike distributive politics, protective-interactive politics involve values that are nontangible. Interaction issues do not raise domestic resource allocation questions. Crises generally, and events properly classed in the arena of protection by their very nature, pertain to the core values of the society.

Finally, there is the fourth arena, termed by Lowi redistributive. As in the regulative arena, politics are conflictual. Indeed, they are highly conflictual. In this political game, the power structure includes both elite and counter-elite. The primary political units either are, or are potentially, classes, movements, generations, nationalities, or other large social aggregates. The phrase ''are potentially'' is not intended to beg the question but merely to indicate that counterelites will speak in the name of, or otherwise attempt to represent themselves as, the defenders of the interests of large social aggregates. In practice they may not succeed in mobilizing these social aggregates—often because the conflict is vigorously suppressed by the elite. The political goods at issue are both tangible and nontangible/symbolic. Consequently, disaggregation is exceedingly limited and difficult. The values at stake, while high, are less central to the core values of a well-integrated society than those at stake in ''protective'' questions, and their impact on society is sharply asymmetrical.

International-National Linkages and the Application of the Issue Area Paradigm

Let us now see how the notion of issue-area based partitions of the policy process can be coupled with that of international-national linkages and transferred from the American pluralist context to Yugoslavia to facilitate our understanding of that country's ''internal'' politics. In the Tito era there was only one really fundamental external challenge of the kind one would associate with the arena of protection and interaction (III) and the policy process we most associate with reactions to external events. That occurred, of course, in 1948 when Stalin attempted to bring down the Tito regime. From what we know [especially Dedijer, 1953], the Yugoslav decisional process reaffirmed the general notion that crisis politics is the same the world around. The decision was taken by a highly legitimate elite acting as individuals, not as institutional representatives, and team norms obtained. (The major exception to this statement, of course, is that a few Yugoslav communist leaders—Andrija Hebrang being the most well known—opted for Stalin and the Cominform rather than Tito and Yugoslavia.)

More revealing about the nexus between international-national linkages and the evolving game of politics in Yugoslavia are three incidents which occurred in the three-year ''Yugoslav crisis'' period (1969-1972). Each corresponds to one of the three cells in the paradigm that are usually associated with domestic politics. The first of these was prompted by the availability of resources from outside Yugoslavia and corresponds quite nicely to the political process associated with the arena of regulation (II).

I refer to what in Yugoslavia is known as the road affair. (For a more detailed treatment, see Burg, 1983, pp. 88-100.) Over the years the International Bank for Reconstruction and Development (IBRD) has provided substantial funds to Yugoslavia for infrastructural support. One form this support has taken has been the provision of extensive grants for road construction, generally amounting to 40 percent of the total cost. "The priority list of roads to be financed by a foreign creditor is usually formulated after a preliminary agreement between the federal government and republics has been reached" [RFE *Research*, August 1, 1969, p. 2]. On this occasion, in 1969, that procedure was not followed completely. Moreover, the substantive outcome was one in which identifiable actors were indulged and others were denied. Specifically, the Slovenians, who according to several Yugoslav journalistic accounts [*Borba*, May 23, 1969; *Ekonomska politika*, January 20, 1969] had evidently thought they were to be among the recipients of funds from the IBRD, were not included. (It should be noted that in 1969 virtually every tourist coming to Yugoslavia by car entered the country through Slovenia.) What appears to have happened was that the Federal Executive Council, viewing the individual road projects as entities to be dispensed, concluded that some of the projects could be funded while others could not. Just as some get liquor licenses in Ann Arbor and some do not, some Yugoslavs were indulged and some were not, and the conflictual politics that implies rapidly became manifest. *Politika* nicely summarizes what happened:

> The decision of the Federal Executive Committee . . . has evoked unbroken waves of protest in all regions of Slovenia. At extraordinary sessions of *opstina* assemblies (in which republic and federal representatives and representatives of social political organizations took part) *opstinas* of Celje, Sentjur, and Slovenske Konjice decided to send protest letters to the Republic Assembly, the Republic Executive Committee, and the Federal Executive Committee demanding that the decision be changed as soon as possible, in view of the great importance of the road for the economy not only of Slovenia but for the whole country as well. Similar protest meetings [*protestni mitinzi*] are being held in many *kolektivs* along the Slovenian coast . . . and today before noon extraordinary sessions of the *opstina* assemblies in Slovenska Bistrica, Maribor, Ajdovscina, and Nova Gorica also led to very sharp protests and even to proposals that the Slovenian federal representatives resign if the FEC's decision is not changed [July 31, 1968].

An international-national linkage had set off a process resembling in many respects regulatory politics as usually depicted by the pressure-group theorists. This was illustrated vividly by the assessment of the affair given by Kardelj himself:

> In recent years we have in fact been witnesses to a growing wave of various pressures. . . . For a time most of the pressures were in the framework of our political system, or at least within certain limits of

tolerance. . . . In a sense the highway campaign was the straw that broke the camel's back. . . . Now let us answer the assertion that the methods were condemned in a sweeping manner, that pressure supposedly already existed, and that the meetings of the *opstina* assemblies in which the highway dispute was taken under consideration constituted a normal form of democratic expression of opinion. . . . It is not merely meetings of *opstina* assemblies that are involved but above all what preceded them and followed them [*Komunist*, October 2, 9, 29, 30, 1969 in *FBIS*, November 21, 1969].

In the road affair, a resource extracted from the outside initiated a process that resulted in a regulatory decision in which groups were deprived. Burg's conclusion is completely in keeping with the implications of our paradigm for the impact of perceived asymmetry on the intensity of conflict: "The Slovene road-building crisis demonstrates clearly that a policy decision that affects the constituent groups in a multinational state *unequally*, can aggravate internationality tensions even when made by an institution constructed on the basis of mutually agreed-on formulas of representation and participation and operating according to mutually agreed-on rules of procedure" [p. 69; italics added]. The substantive and procedural dimension of that decision in turn set into motion a process which, while initially almost classically illustrative of pressure-group politics, had *incipiently* all the qualities of politics in the arena of redistribution: an ethnically cohesive mass available for mobilization, a counterelite willing to advocate the dissolution of Yugoslavia, and high conflict.

By contrast, the second episode, the sudden growth of nationalism in Croatia in 1970-1971 that culminated in the November 1971 student strike at Zagreb University, was an event in which all those attributes were actually present. The story has been told in far greater detail elsewhere [Singleton, 1976, pp. 224-227; Rusinow, 1977, pp. 273-318; Burg, 1983, pp. 121-167]. It suffices here to recount enough of the details to grasp the issues and the nature of the political process. For a combination of reasons, a burgeoning of Croatian national awareness took place in the 1970s. The reasons included the impact of the reforms adopted in the mid-1960s, the genuine devolution of political power from the Federation to the republics, the low birth rate of the Croatian population, and the increased linkages to the outside world. By 1970-1971, the national awareness had begun to be harnessed by potential counterelites in the Croatian cultural organization, Matica Hrvatska, and by those among the more nationalistically inclined leadership in the LC Croatia, Miko Tripalo and Savka Dapcevic-Kucar, in particular. A focus of the discontent was the foreign currency regime which provided that only a small fraction (10 percent) of hard currency earnings could be retained by the enterprises that earned the *valuta*, the remainder being deposited in the federal banks located in Belgrade—the federal capital and the capital of Serbia. Croatians perceived as exceedingly discriminatory the fact that the enterprise that earned the *valuta* could retain such a small percentage. Here was a typical instance of a cleavage between those who demand the money and those who provide the services. People from Croatia, and Croatians generally (many ethnic Croats abroad are from Bosnia) represented at this juncture a disproportionately large fraction of those working abroad and sending remittances back to the country. A disproportionately large share of Croatian industry is highly export oriented, and a disproportionately high share of foreign tourist expenditures occur in Croatia.

This discontent reached a climax in the fall of 1971 (while Tito was in the U. S. negotiating to increase the amount of American investment in the Yugoslav economy). In November 1971 students in Zagreb went on strike in protest against the foreign exchange system. There then followed in quick order a major confrontation between Tito and the Croatian leadership, the purge of the Croatian leadership, and the arrest and incarceration of hundreds of Croatian nationalists. Tito was subsequently to declare that if he had not moved vigorously ''shooting and civil war would perhaps have started in six months' time and you know what that would have meant'' [*Borba*, December 19, 1971].

Whether civil war or shooting would have occurred, we will never know. What we can say is that this was one of the defining events in the history of communist Yugoslavia, an event that bore all the earmarks of the conflictual politics associated with the arena of redistribution (IV). If the result was not civil war, the actors in the process nevertheless were clearly the large social aggregates of which great sociopolitical dramas are made. Indeed, there were many public utterances, most importantly by Savka Dapcevic-Kucar and Miko Tripalo of the LC Croatian party leadership, referring to the emergence of a Croatian national mass *movement*—thus evoking the first South Slav national awakening, the Illyrian movement. There existed a counterelite made up of Croatian nationalists outside the Croatian communist leadership who were powerful enough to demand that the Croatian communist leadership join them if it wished to retain their support. In the words of Drazen Budisa, the president of the Zagreb Union of Students, the political leadership of Croatia must ''place itself at the head of the emerging movement. Our communist leadership, *provided that it desires to be this in the future*, must not settle accounts with our movement concerning a different approach to political tactics'' [*Studentski list*, November 26, 1971; italics added].

There were, moreover, not merely off-the-record mumblings—as there had been in the road affair—to the effect that Croatia would be better off outside the Federation, but instead public demands of which the following were representative: "We wish to free Croatia of her colonial position" [*Studentski list*]; "SR Croatia as a state [should] be admitted to the United Nations"; "Let us form a National Bank and immediately appoint its governor and let us send him to Washington for credits" [Hrvoje Sosic as reported in *Politika*, November 1, 1971]; "We will no longer give our foreign exchange resources"; "The free utilization of foreign exchange resources . . . would make it possible for Croatia to achieve a growth rate of 12-15 percent and to catch up with Sweden in many respects in its economic development during the coming ten years" [Vladimir Veselica in *Borba*, November 21, 1971]. In short, Josip Vrhovec (Secretary of the Executive Committee, LC Croatia) was not engaging in hyperbole when he declared this was "a counterrevolution . . . founded on the concept of a national movement" [*Borba*, January 11, 1972].

Unlike the road affair or the Croatian crisis, the third episode is not portentous. It is illustrative, however, of how an event originating in the external environment can set in motion the kind of pork barrel politics which in the United States we associate with the low-conflict arena of distribution (1). It also is representative of numerous other instances in the 1970s of "formula" politics in Yugoslavia. In 1972, a small ($7.5 million) grant under the United Nations development plan was given to Yugoslavia for the 1972-1976 period. The problem faced by the Yugoslav decisionmakers was as obvious as it was real: how should the funds be allocated? The kind of politics predicted of the arena of distribution envisages a process resulting in a low-conflict, relatively consensual outcome in which everyone that counted politically was cut in. I know of nothing to suggest that the decision taken was controversial. It may have been, but I saw nothing in the Yugoslav press to suggest that it was—whereas other cases that were controversial were widely reported in the press. The decision itself can only be described as inspired. To appreciate fully the decision, the reader must bear in mind two elementary facts about Yugoslavia.

1). There is considerable asymmetry in the level of development among the republics and autonomous regions. In 1970, annual gross social product per capita—a concept differing slightly from gross national product per capita—was $999 for Yugoslavia as a whole and for Serbia proper, "narrow" Serbia. Among the republics, the range extended from 182 percent of the Yugoslav mean for Slovenia and 123 percent for Croatia, to 65 percent, 68 percent and 73 percent for Montenegro, Macedonia, and Bosnia-Hercegovina respectively. Of the two autonomous provinces, Vojvodina had an average income per capita of 119 percent of the Yugoslav mean, while Kosovo was by far the poorest of all the major political units, with only 34 percent of the national average—a mere $340 per capita.

2). The republics vary considerably in population. There are three relatively large republics: Bosnia-Hercegovina, Croatia, and Serbia proper. According to the 1971 census, Bosnia-Hercegovina had a population of approximately 3.74 million; the population of Croatia was roughly 4.43 million, and that of Serbia without the autonomous provinces, 5.25 million. Macedonia and Slovenia were roughly similar in size, Slovenia having approximately 1.71 million and Macedonia 1.65 million. Montenegro is the smallest, with only slightly more than .5 million population; the populations of Vojvodina and Kosovo were estimated at 1.95 and 1.24 million respectively [see Table 3.2].

Imagine yourself in a committee composed of representatives of each republic and region. You are presented with the following allocation and are invited to quickly present an alternative which appeals to a larger coalition than does the following. As reported in *Borba* [January 27, 1972], Bosnia-Hercegovina received 20 percent; Croatia 18 percent; Macedonia 9 percent; Montenegro 8.5 percent; Slovenia, 8.5 percent; Serbia proper 18 percent; and the autonomous provinces, Vojvodina and Kosovo, received 7 percent and 11 percent respectively. Slovenia, with two-and-a-half times the income per capita and population, and Montenegro each received the same shares, thus subsidizing Montenegro while maintaining hypothetical parity between the two. All the republics received more than the autonomous region of Vojvodina. Vojvodina and Kosovo together got as much as did either Serbia proper or Croatia. Croatia and Serbia proper received the same amount.

TABLE 3.2

Comparison of Gross Social Product, Population, and Grant Allocation

Republic or Autonomous Region	% GSP Per Capita	1971 Population in Millions	U.N. Grant Allocation in %
Bosnia-Hercegovina	73	3.746	20
Croatia	123	4.426	18
Macedonia	68	1.647	9
Montenegro	65	.530	8.5
Slovenia	182	1.725	8.5
SR Serbia			
Serbia proper	100	5.250	18
Kosovo	34	1.244	11
Vojvodina	119	1.953	7

SOURCES: for GSP, Vinski [1971], p. 27; for population, *Statisticki godisnjak Jugoslavije*, 1972; for grant allocation, *Borba*, January 27, 1972.

Greater Serbia (SR Serbia), on the other hand, obtained twice that of Croatia, which was in turn offset by the fact that Bosnia-Hercegovina—so dear to the heart of the Croatian nationalists—obtained the largest share of all.

Consequently, while relatively speaking there were winners and losers, no one was totally deprived; rather, everyone who counted politically was cut in. (Note, though, that it is not clear what happened to the funds after they were distributed, and it appears that the actors were not enterprises but the republics and autonomous provinces; whether the republics were fronting particular enterprises in this instance is not known, but seems rather unlikely.) Indeed, the distribution was keenly sensitive to what may fairly be said to be the Yugoslav rules of the game: symbolic parity for republics; regard for Kosovo as a special case; greater benefits and roles for republics than for autonomous provinces, except with regard to development funds for Kosovo; and parity for Croatia and Serbia. As a political good, money has the marvelous quality of being readily disaggregated, and hence the politics of distribution.

CONSOCIATIONAL AUTHORITARIANISM: AN INSTITUTIONAL STRATEGY FOR COHESION AND CONFLICT RESOLUTION

These three cases were not chosen casually. To the old query "Of what are these cases?" an answer for the road affair and the Croatian crisis is that between 1969 and 1972 these were the only two instances when the central party executive organs discussed developments within a single republic. Both were occasions where a strong international-national nexus was present. Both episodes seem to have had considerable impact on the thinking of the Yugoslav leadership. The institutional developments of the early 1970s may be seen, from the perspective of the paradigm articulated here, as efforts to minimize the occurrence of either conflictual policy process, the redistributive arena (IV) or the regulatory arena (II). (Some issues, it should be stressed, are fundamentally intractable to such a strategy, regardless of institutional tinkering. In the Yugoslav setting, for instance, the long-running controversy over funds for developing regions inevitably involves the kind of zero-sum and conflictual politics typical of the arenas of regulation and redistribution. In such cases about the most elites can accomplish is the minimization of nontangible, symbolic issues in such a way that the conflict focuses largely on tangible political goods.) It is an open question whether, had an external threat like Stalin's 1948 attack on Tito occurred in 1970, there existed the national integration required for crisis behavior to correspond to the process I associate with the arena of protection and interaction. The rekindling of Leninist symbols, the ouster of popular republic party leaders in Croatia and Serbia (and in Slovenia and Macedonia as well), and

61

the purging of the press forcibly achieved that reintegration. The Zagreb strike served to remind Yugoslav elites of what could happen when the masses were mobilized by counterelites; and greater media control, it was thought [Bilic, *Tanjug* in *FBIS*, March 21, 1978, pp. I 10-11] would make such an occurrence less likely. The new constitution, the delegate system, and the evolving notion of the State Presidency were designed to strengthen the ethnically defined consociational basis of Yugoslav decisionmaking. For years, Yugoslavia had had its share of pork barrel: rather than build a single large shipyard in Rijeka that could compete internationally, three small ones were built—in Rijeka, in Koper in Slovenia, and in Bar in the south. Decentralization, absent democratization, coupled with the movement away from the market to the preeminence of the "political factor," had the effect of minimizing the likelihood that regulatory politics, with its clear implication of hard, economically rational resource allocation decisions, would occur. After the road affair, the Yugoslavs throughout the 1970s seemed bent on preventing the politically dangerous recurrence of economic rationality. Instead, the strategy of consociational authoritarianism was intended to provide an institutional setup in which resource allocation decisions would neither take on the symbolic coloring that would lead to redistributive politics, nor to regulatory politics with its concomitant clear-cut tangible winners and losers.

In that respect, the small vignette concerning the handling of the U.N. development fund loan was typical of the "formula" politics that characterized much of the Yugoslav game of politics throughout the 1970s and into the post-Tito era. (For multiple examples not involving international-national linkages, see Burg, 1983, passim.) That game was one where all the players that count—read: largely the republican and provincial party organizations—cut themselves in through some kind of formula, most frequently six-sixths or eight-eighths, but sometimes, as in this instance, on a more complicated basis. If, in a particular instance, the players were not cut in, another operative principle characteristic of the pork barrel politics of the arena of distribution was frequently manifest—namely, logrolling. Burg reports a member of the leadership of the Chamber of Republics and Provinces as having said in mid-1976 that situations involving logrolling had arisen " 'only in cases when the acceptance of the position of one delegation on a concrete issue has been conditioned by reciprocal support for the position of another delegation, also on some concrete issue' " [p. 276], but the incidence was, in fact, as Burg observes, much greater. (For a minor and slightly humorous but relevant example of logrolling and Yugoslav ties to the international system, see *Borba* [June 17, 1982, *FBIS*, June 30, 1982, p. I 23], which reports Vojvodina's willingness to accept a social accord on the financing of the Winter Olympics in Sarajevo, Bosnia-Hercegovina, "on the condition that [there be adopted] a social accord on financing the world table tennis championship which was held in Novi Sad [the capital of Vojvodina] last year.")

In short, the changes promulgated after the road affair and the Croatian crisis may be seen as efforts to provide an institutional setting in which the policy processes associated with the arena of distribution—logrolling, *unprincipled* alliances of uncommon interests, and a nonconflicting elite with support groups—or the arena of protection and interaction—a highly legitimate elite acting as individuals "without their institutions" and playing by team norms—would prevail. By the same note, the two conflictual arenas of power, the arena of regulation—with its pluralist and multicentered coalitions based on shared interests—and the arena of redistribution where movements, classes or generations were the main players and the power structure involved both elites and counterelites, were to be avoided as much as possible.

As manifested in practice there were two major levels to this strategy for cohesion and conflict resolution. One was the blend of harmonization/decentralization and re-Leninization that constituted consociational authoritarianism as it was played out among the republics at the federal level. The other was the way consociational authoritarianism resulted in ambiguity in the Yugoslav constitutional and institutional order as it evolved in the 1970s pertaining to the relation between the autonomous provinces and the Republic of Serbia.

THE FAILURE OF THE CONSOCIATIONAL STRATEGY: KOSOVO, 1977-1984

From 1968 to 1981 the trend was unmistakably in the direction of minimizing the differences between republics and provinces—for the six to be viewed as the eight. We now know that, dating from 1976 on, there has been enormous interelite controversy across a wide range of key issues involving the Republic of Serbia, Vojvodina, and Kosovo. From the perspective of the Serbian party and governmental leadership, the issues involved "the permanent escalation of demands for the transfer of competence to the Socialist Autonomous Regions in the areas of citizenship, security, statistics, planning, or in the case of the League of Communists, demands that the provincial committees be called Central Committees, and provincial conferences—Congresses of the League of Communists" [Dragoslav Markovic in *NIN*, May 17, 1981, p. 10]. One may properly take a somewhat jaundiced stance about Markovic's implied views on the merits of the issues, but he has the categories right and for that matter the direction of the trend during Tito's last years.

From 1977 to 1982-1983 there existed a virtual stalemate between the leaderships of Serbia, Kosovo, and Vojvodina. The social plan could not be negotiated. The secret police were not sharing information. Statistics could not be gathered for the whole republic. "It is well known that in the Republic [of Serbia] to now [1981—the bill was finally passed in 1982] the National Defense Law has not been ratified inasmuch as its shaping has just begun. All other republics have adopted such laws. It is no secret that the main reason for this delay is the dispute again about competencies and jurisdiction" [NIN, May 17, 1981, p. 11]. The extent to which the stalemate had gone is nicely illustrated by another NIN article, this one on April 3, 1983:

> Well, we are entering in the sixth year since one lives in Serbia virtually—illegally. It is exactly that much time since the abandonment of the old federal law on citizenship. Until 1979, Serbia did not have a republic law, and so its 10 million inhabitants had neither republic nor Yugoslav citizenship since the first was precondition for the second. Even more recently, when the content of the law on citizenship was accepted, the tension between the republic and the provinces continued over the question: who gives and takes away citizenship, the republic or the provincial [authorities]?
>
> How much longer will this illegal situation last? The answer is—until yesterday. The day before the appearance of this number of NIN on the newsstands, the Parliament of Serbia finally passed a republic law" [NIN, p. 18].

Virtually all these issues were dividing the leaderships of the provinces and the republic in 1977, though knowledge of this reality was closely kept within the republic and federal leadership. ("The whole truth . . . is to be found in several thousand pages of stenographic reports which are still under 'embargo.' Whether or not this material will be published or made available to the broad public is difficult to say" [NIN, May 17, 1981, p. 10].) The picture of a relatively harmonious politics largely given over to trading votes and making deals over tangible matters turns out to describe only a part of the game of politics in the last years of the Tito era, though party control of the media kept the public from being informed *or* mobilized. Indeed, Najdan Pasic contended in 1981 that it was the fear of really major conflict that prevented any effort to resolve the controversies. "We capitulated before our own kind of political opportunism. The fear of some open political confrontation resulted in it [the dispute] being simply removed from the agenda" [NIN, May 17, 1981, p. 13].

The outcomes of the interelite controversy involving tangible and key symbolic issues became clear only in the aftermath of the riots in Kosovo in 1981. These riots were a replay, magnified in intensity, of the 1968 disturbances which resulted when Serbian dominance in Kosovo was reduced following the ouster of Rankovic, for whom Kosovo had been a virtual fiefdom. (See Rusinow's depiction of 1968, especially p. 245.) The underlying causes of the riots were obvious. Both Serbs and Albanians have enormous emotional ties to Kosovo. The interwar experience was one of Serbian colonization and enormous resentment of Yugoslavia by the Albanians in Kosovo—a resentment which was manifest in World War II, and in the early postwar period. The domination of Kosovo by Rankovic and the Serbs very likely was not perceived by Albanians in Kosovo as being fundamentally different from interwar Serbian rule. The population of Kosovo is overwhelmingly (78 percent) Albanian. After Rankovic's ouster, there was a noticeable trend toward the Albanianization of the political leadership, and enormous development of institutions—the university, the status of the autonomous provinces in the federal scheme, and the Constitution of 1974—that symbolized and increased identification with Kosovo. Nevertheless, unemployment increased rapidly from an already high 18.6 percent in 1971 to 27.5 percent by 1981. (See for more detail, Baskin, 1983, pp. 61-74; Banac in Vucinich, ed., 1982.)

As Table 3.3, shows, the distribution of wealth across regions in Yugoslavia has evolved steadily in the direction of less equality over the entire post-World War II period. While the lot of everyone in Yugoslavia has improved immensely, the gap between Slovenia and Kosovo has grown steadily. (The main reason for this is differential population growth rates.) The student population in Kosovo has become very large; unfortunately, they have usually been taught in Albanian and trained in the social sciences. In a region where unemployment was increasing, in circumstances where the gap between that region and others was growing, and where there existed an alternative nation state, however repressive, outside Yugoslavia with which the university in Pristina had close ties, the students were readily available for mobilization, lacking only, as Lenin would have put it, a spark.

The political process which followed was precisely what one would expect of the arena of redistribution. While some protestors termed themselves "the children of Skenderbeg, the army of Enver Hoxha" and shouted "Long live Marxism—down with revisionism," and some claimed "We are Albanians, not Yugoslavs," and others demanded "Union with Albania," the far more prevalent theme was symbolic and tangible equality within Yugoslavia: hence the slogan "Kosovo-Republic" or simply, "K-R." Counterelites formed, including 33 illegal groups in Kosovo and a handful of others in places in Macedonia where there are sizable concentrations of Albanians. *NIN* tells us there had been a major upsurge in the activities of the "pro-Albanian emigration" abroad and that there were ties between the emigrant organization, the Red National Front, and such groups

TABLE 3.3
Yugoslav Social Product Per Capita in Percentages (Yugoslav mean = 100%)

Republic or Autonomous Region	1947	1953	1960	1965	1970
Bosnia-Hercegovina	85.8	85.7	76.0	71.7	67.6
Croatia	104.6	115.4	115.6	120.3	123.6
Macedonia	70.3	65.9	63.9	66.6	70.0
Montenegro	93.7	74.8	64.5	76.3	77.2
Slovenia	162.1	161.1	180.5	183.1	193.7
SR Serbia					
Serbia proper	100.5	96.8	96.5	96.3	96.5
Kosovo	49.3	45.8	37.4	36.5	34.1
Vojvodina	99.6	99.4	108.0	112.5	107.4

Republic or Autonomous Region	1975	1977	1979	1981	1983
Bosnia-Hercegovina	65.8	65.1	64.6	67.0	68.6
Croatia	123.1	124.8	125.9	126.2	124.8
Macedonia	68.0	68.1	67.4	66.0	65.2
Montenegro	69.1	71.1	66.1	78.4	77.0
Slovenia	205.2	200.2	205.8	196.3	197.0
SR Serbia					
Serbia proper	96.7	98.5	99.6	98.0	99.0
Kosovo	33.4	30.4	28.2	29.3	27.9
Vojvodina	115.1	117.6	115.2	119.7	120.6

SOURCES: For 1947-1979, Mladenovic [1979], p. 9; for 1981-1983, *Statisticki godisnjak Jugoslavije*, 1984.

in Kosovo as the "Group of Marxist-Leninists in Kosovo" and the "Kosovan National Liberation Movement" [*NIN*, April 2, 1982, p. 8]. More ominously from the Serbian and even the Yugoslav point of view, there were reports in the Belgrade press about connections between the leadership in Kosovo at the time of the riots and those arrested.

The reaction of the Federation to the riots was swift; "a state of emergency" was declared, a curfew imposed, army units were mobilized and brought into the Kosovo from outside, and virtual martial law imposed. The subsequent reaction by the Serbian republic leadership—supported by the "broad masses" of Serbs including liberal intellectuals, my conversations in Belgrade in January 1983 suggest—was equally intense and purposeful. In Kosovo there exists enormous resentment of a situation in which the disparity between the poorer and wealthier regions is immense and has not been narrowed, and where Kosovo is denied the status which would represent symbolic equality.

The resentment in Kosovo is matched by the hostility among Serbs toward Albanians. There is a widespread feeling that the Albanians are in-grates and that the slogan "Kosovo-Republic," however odious, is but a step to an ethnically homogenous Albanian republic. Such a republic would not be limited to Kosovo alone, but would embrace all the areas in Yugoslavia where Albanians are in the majority and would envisage Kosovo as the Piedmont of a greater Albania made up of all Albanians from Yugoslavia and from Albania itself. The result has been, aside from highly repressive measures directed against ordinary Kosovars, especially the young, a conscious and extensive campaign by the Serbian leadership to reassert its preeminence over the entire republic, including "narrow" Serbia, Kosovo *and* Vojvodina, and to reverse the trend of many years' standing in the direction of blurring the differences between autonomous province and republic status. Instead, the Serbian leadership is aggressively emphasizing the differences.

This has produced agreements favoring the republic in many areas where the question of the division of competence between the republic and the provinces had been at issue or even settled in favor of the provinces. In 1983, Serbia and Montenegro launched a campaign to diminish the status of the Albanian national flag (Macedonia made a similar attempt in 1981), a campaign which even the leadership of Kosovo opposed. Ismail Bajra, in 1983 a member of the "chairmanship" of the provincial LC, stated that "A component part of the expression of national individuality and the implementation of the policy of national equality [is] the free and equal use of national flags of the nations and nationalities throughout our multinational Yugoslav Federation. The free and equal use of the national flags of the nations and nationalities reflects the strengthening of the cohesion and unity of our country. Only the unitarists, the *etatists* and state nationalists can claim . . . that the national flags of the nationalities, and in particular that of the Albanians, allegedly threaten the unity and the state, the sovereignty and the integrity of the Yugoslav Federation" [*Rilindja*, February 22, 1983, in RFE *Research*, March 14, 1983, pp. 3-4]. Finally, the Serbian leadership and media have vociferously attacked the outmigration of non-Albanians from Kosovo by giving enormous publicity to ethnic incidents that spark departures and to the occasional return of an ethnically Serbian or Montenegrin family to Kosovo. (On the "tipping" process whereby communities become segregated racially, see Thomas Schelling [1981], who suggests that the phenomenon is a far more automatic and less conscious process.) In short, in the aftermath of the 1981 mass riots in Kosovo, a fundamentally redistributive process, especially with respect to symbolic questions and questions of jurisdiction, has been undertaken. The scarcely disguised intent of that process is to keep the Albanians in their place and to assert the claim that republic status for Kosovo would be fatal for the Federation because it would lead inevitably to Kosovo's secession and the breakup of Yugoslavia. That matters had—whether we believe this to be a valid projection or not—come to such a pass was in large part a product of Tito's effort to provide symbolic concessions, just short of republic status, to Kosovo and Vojvodina in the 1970s. "The consociational legitimation of subcultures" [Baskin, 1983] can create as well as solve conflict, and in this context consociational authoritarianism has enhanced, rather than obviated, the prospects that the game of politics in Yugoslavia will involve the conflict between social movements or nationalities we associate with the arena of redistribution.

POLITICS IN A ZERO-SUM SOCIETY: INTERNATIONAL-NATIONAL LINKAGES AND THE FEDERATION, 1979-1984

Consociational authoritarianism has been a more successful strategy for national cohesion as the game of politics has been played at the level of the Federation. Here too, though, while governance has been possible, the results have produced political processes that have differed on several occasions from what was expected. While politically attractive, especially, but not only, in ethnically diverse polities, consociational authoritarianism is economically inefficient. It creates an environment in which domestic and foreign investments are sought for politically attractive, but economically irresponsible, purposes. It encourages and rewards a strategy that implies republic or republic and provincial autarky, with corresponding decisions to create or to seek to create multiple electronics industries, shipbuilding facilities, airlines, nuclear power stations and the like without regard for economies of scale. While Yugoslav economists are eloquent in condemning such practices, Yugoslav political elites clearly choose to pursue such a course as a political tactic, to use a favored Yugoslav phrase, in order to "keep peace in the family." When coupled with the exogenous shock of the energy crisis as its ramifications worked their way through the Yugoslav economy, the economic costs of the mechanism proved overwhelming. By the end of the Tito era, and continuing into the 1980s, the Yugoslavs found themselves increasingly in situations where "harmonization" has proved impossible to achieve.

As resources have become scarcer, there has been an increase in occasions where proposed policy changes involve winners and losers. One result is a rise in the number of instances where one or more republic vetoed a proposed act and prevented any action from being taken. Zdenko Antic [RFE *Research*, November 10, 1982, p. 6] provides a partial list of recent such occasions: in 1979 Vojvodina refused to accept the law banning the use of liquid fuel for power plants; in November 1980 Yugoslavia's social plan was not signed because of a lack of agreement; in 1981 Slovenia refused to sign a law providing for a tax for every departure from the country; in January 1982 a scheduled federal price-rise regulation was not signed for lack of agreement. Of these, the Slovenian refusal in 1981 to allow a tax on every departure from the country was most obviously concerned with international-national linkages [*Belgrade domestic*, *FBIS*, July 28, 1981, p. I 8; *Politika*, August 8, 1981, in *FBIS*, August 11, 1981, p. I 4]. Others on Antic's list were as well: thus the balance of payments deficit dispute was closely linked to the 1980 social plan.

Inaction, however, has become a less viable alternative in the context of the deteriorating economic situation—a core element of which has been the $20 billion external debt which is, in turn, partly a product of bad intrarepublic investment decisions. Beginning in 1979, the Federal Executive Committee (FEC) has had to resort to measures that facilitate the making of hard choices even in the face of regional opposition.

A major instance that involved an all-encompassing series of measures occurred in October 1982. On that occasion, the government announced a bevy of measures that would drastically curtail hard currency expenditures: the dinar was devalued, gasoline and diesel fuel rationing was introduced, restrictions on electricity consumption were imposed, the use of foreign currency within the country was restricted, and a "deposit" for each trip abroad which increased in amount per trip was mandated. (The latter was, of course, a tax, given 30 percent inflation.) Several things are striking about the adoption of these measures. Basically, the political processes involved are most analogous to the arena of protection and interaction, as a genuine crisis, even one involving no military threat to national security, should entail. There seems to have been a perception of genuine crisis, sharpened by blackouts and brownouts and shortages of cooking oil, detergent, medicines, gasoline and diesel fuel. The measures were passed quite quickly and with minimum discussion and controversy. As *Politika* put it, even though "such talks and measures require the agreement of a large number of people and institutions . . . the main . . . work was completed virtually in seven days, something that represents an event in our political practice" [*Politika*, October 20, 1982, in *FBIS*, October 28, 1982, pp. I 11-12]. In the FEC, which played a central role in introducing and adopting the measures, team norms obtained: "According to what we hear, any . . . manifestation of affiliation with 'one's own republic or province' is shunned within the Federal Executive Council." With the exception of the deposit (whose impact was manifestly asymmetrical), which produced an extensive reaction in Croatia and Slovenia especially, the measures were carefully designed—again except for the deposit—to pinch everyone more or less equally. There was, as one would expect in a crisis, almost no adverse reaction to the measures unrelated to the deposit; even Milovan Djilas declared the measures "are not bad . . . I as a dissident take a positive attitude vis-à-vis these measures" [Hellfried Brandl interview over Vienna Domestic Service, November 19, 1982, in *FBIS*, November 23, 1982, p. I 5]. As Jure Bilic expressed it in an unusually frank comment on the link between crisis and conflict, "Unity is created in party leaderships when matters get absurd, when it is a matter of do or die. Frankly speaking, it is like that" [*Vjesnik*, December 31, 1982, January 1, 2, 3; *FBIS*, January 17, 1983, p. I 4].

As reference to the deposit intimates, other decisions taken by the government have produced more conflictual politics. Armed with Articles 301, 302, and 303 of the 1974 Yugoslav Constitution, the FEC has made a number of hard choices, and the attendant policy processes have resembled closely those an issue-area paradigm would project for the arena of regulation. To minimize symbolic overtones, the regime tried to shape people's expectations that the deposit was, as the deputy ministry of Foreign Affairs put it, a "purely economic measure" [*Tanjug*, October 22, 1982, in *FBIS*, October 27, 1982, p. I 5]. Similarly, the regime publicly condemned—to little effect—the sudden upsurge in the number of unsanctioned trips abroad: in Ribicic's words, people must "stop to consider [the impact] when they use their authorization for an official trip to go to Trieste to buy themselves some coffee" [*Tanjug*, November 26, 1982, in *FBIS*, November 30, 1982, p. I 4; also Dusan Ckrebic, as reported by *Belgrade domestic*, November 5, 1982, in *FBIS*, November 8, 1982, p. I 9]. Subsequently, the leadership moved rather quickly to loosen the rules on border traffic in order to reduce the hardship on those in Croatia, Slovenia, and Vojvodina most acutely affected by the deposit. All these steps may be seen as efforts to defuse the notion that the deposit had implications for nontangible symbolic values and thus became an issue that would spill over into the redistributional arena. This proved quite a task. The regime has invested enormous efforts in creating the impression that Yugoslavia is an open society. The right to travel is defined as a fundamental attribute of being a Yugoslav by many Yugoslavs, especially, but not only, in Slovenia and Croatia.

For the controversy over the deposit not to take on the redistributive characteristics of symbolic politics, the FEC had to assure various Yugoslav publics that the deposit decision was motivated by economic considerations and would not be asymmetrical in its consequences. What actually followed the October decision was a political process that was highly reminiscent of politics in the arena of regulation in the United States. *Politika* [January 20, 1983] reported that "The Executive Councils of Croatia, Slovenia, and Serbia, as well as several tourist agencies [had] all sent letters about [the decree] to the Federal Executive Council" and that many "citizens have turned to the Yugoslav Supreme Court with a demand that it conduct proceedings and evaluate the constitutionality (*ustavnost*) of the application of the deposit.'' In March 1983, the Slovene Socialist Alliance Conference—despite the FEC's decision of February 10, 1983, to ease local border traffic restrictions—wrote a letter (which *Borba* [!] described as containing ''several soundly argued political and economic reasons'') to the FEC that characterized the overall policy concerning the deposit as a ''blow to Yugoslavia as a country of open borders'' [*Borba*, March 31, 1983, in *FBIS*, April 11, 1983, p. I 12], and called for the elimination of all restrictions on local border traffic. Obviously concerned lest such opposition become intensified, the FEC backtracked. In December 1983 the FEC decided to retain the deposit, but to allow, effective January 1, 1984, all Yugoslav citizens an annual exemption and to exempt totally ''citizens who are temporarily employed abroad and members of their immediate family . . . citizens who visit members of their immediate family who are permanent residents abroad . . . holders of border area passes . . . and people with dual citizenship'' [*Tanjug*, in *FBIS*, December 30, 1983, p. I 12]. At the end of 1984 the deposit requirement was abandoned.

Balance of payments problems and rules concerning the retention of hard currency have produced similar conflict patterns with slightly different institutional mechanisms. In 1979 the FEC resorted to invoking Articles 301 and 302 of the 1974 Constitution in order to grapple with Yugoslavia's balance of payments deficit. The measure proposed had the effect, in the eyes of the Slovenian and Croatian delegations to the *Skupstina*, of placing the burden for reducing the envisaged deficit by $500 million dollars (*not* dinars) on the developed republics. The Slovenes flatly opposed the proposed solution, while the Croatians took a less hostile, but nevertheless negative, stance. According to Burg [1983, p. 294] in order to pass the social plan for 1980, ''the Federal Executive Committee . . . decided in December [1979] to begin the process of proposing a temporary measure to limit the deficit for 1980. Unofficially, all agreed that negotiations would resume again in January. Final agreement on a permanent solution was not reached until August [1980].'' In a third example, again with a strong international-national linkage, it appears that the FEC threatened to invoke Articles 301 and 302, this time in 1982. In a manner reminiscent of 1971 in Croatia, the issue was again the *valuta* retention rules. After much bargaining and great controversy [*Borba*, April 7, 1982, in *FBIS*, April 15, 1982, p. I 4; *Tanjug* in *FBIS*, April 28, 1982, p. I 20; *Tanjug*, May 10, 1982, in *FBIS*, May 11, 1982], the regions agreed to a modified law as a temporary measure on the last day of the parliamentary session [*Tanjug*, *FBIS*, May 12, 1982, in *FBIS*, May 13, 1982, p. I 3] after concessions were made to Slovenia and Croatia. Once again, as in the balance of payments example, the leaders of the developed republics seem to have felt they were being ganged up on. Unlike the balance of payments dispute and much like the 1969 Slovene road affair, the dispute had incipiently the symbolic qualities of the redistributive arena. There were utterances in Croatia that paralleled the themes of the 1971 Croatian mass movement [Zlatko Uzelac, as cited in *Tanjug*, in *FBIS*, March 29, 1982, p. I 3]. But for the Croatian leaders the issue seems, in this instance, to have been limited to money and the politics of regulation (arena II).

What all this suggests is that, at the outset of the 1980s, as at the outset of the 1970s, economic resources external to Yugoslavia were having a profound effect on the game of politics in Yugoslavia. In each of the three instances we have examined in this chapter, there has been the real possibility that the issues could provoke the mobilization of masses by regional elites, but this has largely not happened thus far. At the same time, the whole system of harmonization of interests has been called into question by events. The effort to avoid conflict, as a systematic strategy, has had to yield to the more pressing need to address the economic exigencies that are a direct result of policy choices concerning how Yugoslavia shall link with the global economy.

It is difficult not to stress that the first occasion in which the FEC had to resort to the fail-safe procedures for governance in the absence of agreement concerned the balance of payments. It is similarly hard not to note that the muted recurrence of the mass-movement theme related in the early 1980s, as in the early 1970s, to the disposition of hard currency by enterprises. In an economy of scarcity, politics as usual, Yugoslav style—what we have called the politics of distribution, with its characteristic logrolling and coalitions of the *unlike*-minded, and what the Yugoslavs call harmonization— is almost certain to fail.

Except in genuine crises, the trend in the Yugoslav game of politics in the near term at the Federation level will be to downplay ''harmonization'' and to resort increasingly to the hard choices and to zero-sum politics of the arena of regulation with majority and minority coalitions of the like-minded. Institutionally, the economic realities are likely to produce intensified demands for increased centralization as between the political and regional centers, with it being up for grabs whether such centralization implies an increased or a decreased trend toward democratization, and whether a trend toward centralization among the political units will be accompanied by devolution of decisionmaking to enterprises and the market. Indeed, the political dialogue between 1982 and 1984 was preoccupied with exactly such issues. In sharp contrast to relations involving the status of the autonomous provinces both within the Republic of Serbia and in the Federation, the issues concerning the republics and their relation to the international economy have managed largely to avoid the mobilization of large social groups we associate with the arena of redistribution. There have been several issues directly involving international linkages—balance of payments, the disposition of hard currency, the deposit—that smack potentially of such highly conflictual politics, but the mobilization of mass publics has thus far not occurred. (It is fear of this possibility and of political changes that would weaken the position of the republic party organs and the republic leaders that seems to have prompted the effort, to little apparent avail, to harness, once again, the Belgrade and Zagreb press in the spring 1983.)

Whether the lack of mass mobilization will persist is quite contingent. Yugoslavia, like the rest of the world, might get a little lucky: the global economy may revive for some period of time and there may be less need to make hard choices. The leadership may continue to make hard choices. In so doing it may demonstrate that a policy process that entails principled coalitions need not involve consistent cleavages, but may rather involve the kinds of crosscutting cleavages that pluralist politics implies normatively. Fortunately, the 1974 Constitution created mechanisms that allow both for consensus and for majority rule in the absence of such consensus.

For that to happen, however, Yugoslav elites must be able to convince themselves and their constituents in their respective republics that the primary rationale for the choices being made is economic not political, and that whatever administrative measures are adopted are prompted by similar concerns. In Yugoslavia in the 1980s, it is necessary for economic measures with clearly asymmetrical consequences to be, and be seen to be, temporary. Some kinds of political reforms and changes in institutions that have the effect of reducing the domain of politics and the power of republic party organizations are also implied. We have seen that absent a crisis, Yugoslav elites have, where possible, shunned economic rationality and the political processes of the arena of regulation like the plague for the conflict-minimizing and economically expensive arena of distribution. Some of the impetus for a greater disposition—all political systems require some modicum of logrolling and patronage as grease—toward regulatory rather than distributive politics may come from actors external to Yugoslavia: German, American, and other multinational firms, Western banks, the IMF, and the United States government.

4

OPENING THE BORDERS:
YUGOSLAV MIGRANT WORKERS AND THE
INTERNATIONAL MARKET

Chapters 2 and 3 revealed how closely Yugoslavia has paralleled the patterns of power seizure by other "authentic" communist regimes and the extent to which the Yugoslav elite set out systematically to imitate the Soviet model in the years following World War II. The result was a political system that at the time of Stalin's break with Tito in 1948 had acquired all the attributes of a closed political system. Like other communist elites, Yugoslav leaders proceeded to insulate their citizenry from the world outside their country's borders. The leadership revealed its low trust in its citizenry and its concern for control and fear of spontaneity: both the inflow of ideas from outside the territorial boundaries of Yugoslavia and the foreign travel of Yugoslav citizens were strictly regulated. Just as the imposition of a one-party Leninist system with its attendant regime monopoly of the key public agents of political socialization and the absence of competitive parties implied regime-society relations in which the citizenry were denied an effective voice, the rigid demarcation of boundaries bespoke the regime's hostility to exit as well [Hirschman, 1970, and *World Politics*, 1978, pp. 90-108].

The political motivation to insulate the Yugoslav citizenry from outside influences had its counterpart in economic public policy choices that isolated the citizen from external market forces. Autarchy, full employment through mass underemployment, political factories, nationalization, and the expropriation of foreign holdings all signified a determination to sever Yugoslavia's ties to the international market. The first decade after World War II were years in Yugoslavia when, in the words of *Ekonomska politika* [February 24, 1969, in *Joint Translation Service*, February 28, 1969, p. 38], "going to work in a foreign country was treated as well nigh a betrayal" and hence such an action "in practical language . . . meant also political emigration." (These were years, as Belgrade's *Politika* was to remark sarcastically [if appositely] in 1973, "When the obtaining of passports depended on janitors' statements" [March 18, 1973].)

One result, consequently, of the communist seizure of power in Yugoslavia was a profound reorientation in attitudes toward migration. For centuries, South Slavs had viewed population migration as a natural response to economic conditions [Grecic, 1975, p. 193]. There had been a massive transoceanic migration of South Slavs before World War I, and thousands of South Slavs had gone to work in more urbanized and developed parts of Europe, both before World War I and during the interwar period as well. (Tito himself was a guest worker in Austria before World War I.) In the decade after World War II, by contrast, those that went abroad were generally severing their ties with the Yugoslav political system and migrating for reasons that were either political or viewed as being political. Yugoslav sources are vague about the period from 1945 to 1953. We know that the relocation of the boundaries between Italy and Yugoslavia produced a substantial movement of former Yugoslav citizens to Italy. Similarly, there was a massive departure of ethnic Germans in the aftermath of World War II. Whereas there had been approximately a half-million ethnic Germans in Yugoslavia before World War II, the 1948 census reported less than 60,000 who identified themselves as German, and the 1971 census lists slightly more than 13,000 who so characterized themselves. (There may well have been some number of people who remained in Yugoslavia but who no longer wished to be identified as Germans ethnically.)

Until the late 1950s there were only a handful of Yugoslavs abroad for what could be classified as economic reasons. Only very gradually did the decompression in Yugoslav regime-society relations that occurred in other domains as the Yugoslav leadership assimilated the full implications of the Stalin-Tito clash come to have a bearing on the international mobility of Yugoslav workers. There were no explicit changes in the official stance vis-à-vis work abroad. As Ivo Baucic [1979, p. 7], the most careful Yugoslav student of Yugoslav migrations, has noted, "Up to 1962, our social political orientation in relation to departure and work in foreign countries was negative. Departure was neither accepted nor justified. [Rather] it was in contradiction to social-political norms." Concretely, however, in the improved political atmosphere of the late 1950s, more such migration was in practice tolerated than had been previously the case, and beginning in 1954 a trickle of workers (largely Croatian ethnically) began to flow to Western Europe, most notably to the Federal Republic of Germany. In 1954, the first year for which any specific estimates are available, there were fewer than 2,000 Yugoslav workers in Germany and roughly 3,000 in Europe; by 1961, there were 17,800 and 28,000 respectively in Germany and Europe generally. (Baucic, 1979, p. 6).

OPENING THE FLOODGATES

By 1962-1963, the official stance began to change explicitly and openly as part of the general liberalizing orientation of the early 1960s that culminated in the 1965 economic reforms and in the 1966 ouster of Aleksandar Rankovic. By the mid-1960s, public utterances of prominent Yugoslav spokesmen regularly endorsed the outmigration of Yugoslav workers. In 1964, analogous views toward migration were expressed in the Croatian journal *Nase teme* by Zvonimir Baletic, and by Vladimir Bakaric, then a dominant figure in the Croatian party organization, in an interview in Belgrade's *NIN*. Baletic wrote:

> For the individual persons who leave their country to work abroad the benefits are apparent. The very fact that someone wants to live and work abroad indicates that such a person expects to improve his economic position; as a rule, such an improvement takes place. The interests of society can be in opposition to the interests of the individual. Man has the right to seek and find better working and living conditions, to choose the place and milieu in which he would like to live, although society has the right to take measures of self-defense against arbitrary actions of individuals. Both of these rights must be taken into account in formulating an international migration policy [*Nase teme*, 1965, pp. 680-700].

Likewise, in March 1964 Bakaric had stated in response to the questions about Yugoslavs working abroad "privately": "The fact is that . . . it is almost exclusively a Croatian emigration, [composed of] emigration from Croatia and the Croatian parts of Hercegovina. From Croatia, they go mainly from the backward regions, economically backward, where there is no prospect for rapid development. . . . We cannot quickly compete, we cannot achieve a more rapid development in the underdeveloped regions— we do not have the means" [Bakaric, 1967, p. 128].

By the late 1960s, the Yugoslavs had raised the notion of open borders to the level of state policy. Rather than a stance of tolerance or resignation, the open borders policy had come to be identified in official utterances as one of the key defining features, along with market socialism and self-management, of what was distinct and positive in the Yugoslav socialist variant and an element that set off Yugoslavia from the Soviet model. Thus the Yugoslavs could congratulate themselves in 1969 that "The policy of good neighbour relations and 'open boundaries' being pursued by Yugoslavia has yielded valuable positive experience not only as regard the feasibility of fruitful cooperation and peaceful coexistence between states with different social systems, but also at the level of establishing and expanding channels of communication for direct contacts between individuals and nongovernmental groups in society" [Vlado Benko, *Review of International Affairs*, November 20, 1969, p. 4]. Similarly, they cast aspersions on "the contemporary mentality of camp socialism" which is "shocked by the fact that our people are so easily permitted to leave their homeland to return without any prejudices after a few years" [*Borba*, May 17, 1969, in *Joint Translation Service*, May 21, 1969, p. 6].

The shift in political attitudes toward the openness of the country's borders was inextricably linked with the shift in views—a shift which took place first in Slovenia and Croatia and then, with the defeat of Rankovic, throughout the country—concerning Yugoslavia's ties to the international economy and about market relations more broadly. Economists and public figures alike began to refer favorably to the international division of labor, and to a strategy of independence based on a commitment to fostering exports rather than on autarky—phrases that stood for broader economic and political values. An export-based economy participating in the international division of labor would be a more Western oriented economy and, most of the reform advocates hoped (and Rankovic feared), a more Western society and was a necessary concomitant to the devolution of economic decision-making away from the state and the planners to the enterprise and the consumers. Economic decentralization in turn would decentralize power, thus increasing individual freedom—and increasing unemployment—and reducing the likelihood of a resurgence of what in Yugoslav parlance is termed "state socialism."

The attitude shift found institutional expression in policy choices that revealed both a political determination to open the boundaries for all Yugoslavs and a conscious choice of economic policies that would encourage economically induced migration. The 1963 Constitution declared among other things in Article 36 that "The right to work and the freedom to work are guaranteed. . . . Everyone shall be free to choose an occupation and employment." The nearly simultaneous liberalization of the passport service created the political conditions for economically motivated migration; as one Croatian scholar put it, that liberalization made Article 36 "applicable in the region of foreign migration" [Komarica, 1970, p. 104]. From 1963 on, moreover, the Yugoslav Employment Service began to serve as a mediator between foreign employers and employment services and the Yugoslav workers "who were informed of the possibilities of work abroad and who were helped prior to their departure abroad" [Baucic, 1979, p. 8]; and the Yugoslav National Bank began to take separate note of the hard currency remissions of workers abroad and emigrants.

These policy initiatives culminated in those decisions made in connection with the economic reforms in 1965. The economic intent of the reforms (for many, there were political values to be served as well) was to decentralize economic decisions from the planners to the market; to eliminate the immensely inefficient political factories with their attendant underemployment; to encourage the international mobility of resources, both labor and capital, by devaluing the dinar and ultimately making it convertible; and to allow the international market to serve as the efficient allocator of values. With the 1965 reforms, the economic incentives for migration were greatly enhanced. An immediate consequence of economic decentralization was a decrease in the total number employed and an increase in the already-substantial number "of people looking for employment" (to use the circumlocution of the Yugoslav *Statistical Yearbooks*). Where there were 3,662,000 employed in 1965, 4,000 fewer were employed and 20,000 more unemployed in 1966. By 1967, the number employed had decreased to 3,561,000 and the number unemployed had reached 269,100. After 1967 the number of employed increases again, but it is not until 1969 that the number exceeded that in 1965. Meanwhile, the number of unemployed increased steadily between 1965 and 1969, reaching a peak in 1969 and then decreasing somewhat in 1970 and 1971 (see Table 4.1).

Furthermore, the devaluation of the dinar increased the attractiveness of work abroad. Where the prereform rate had been officially 750 dinars to the U.S. dollar, the exchange rate in 1965 was altered to 1,250 to 1. Since there was a wide range of effective rates prior to 1965, it has been argued that part of the devaluation was nominal. Nevertheless, even if the previous "true" rate had been 1,000 dinars to the dollar, the reform implied a 25 percent devaluation in the dinar. Moreover, the higher rates of the old multiple system were far more relevant to the export industries than to the Yugoslav worker. The new dinar exchange rate, in Ivo Vinski's words, "along with stimulating the import of goods and services, stimulated perhaps even more greatly the export of living labor in the sense of the employment of our workers abroad" [*Ekonomski pregled*, July 1971, p. 367].

The changed attitude toward the permeability of the country's boundaries was reflected in the immense growth in the egress and ingress of all persons across Yugoslav borders as well as in the burgeoning number of Yugoslav workers abroad. It is possible to conjure up a scenario in which a receptivity to foreign tourism is compatible with a persisting determination to insulate the citizenry from foreign contacts. Consequently, the increase in foreign

TABLE 4.1
Employed and Unemployed in Yugoslavia, 1964-1971 (In thousands)

Year	Number Employed	Number Unemployed	Year	Number Employed	Number Unemployed
1964	3,608	212.5	1968	3,587	311.0
1965	3,662	237.0	1969	3,706	330.6
1966	3,583	257.6	1970	3,850	319.6
1967	3,561	269.1	1971	4,033	291.3

SOURCE: *Statisticki godisnjak Jugoslavije*, 1984, p. 81.

border crossings into Yugoslavia or the growth of the foreign tourist industry might not be seen as part of a fundamental alteration in elite attitudes or regime-society relations in Yugoslavia absent evidence of a markedly increased proclivity of Yugoslavs for foreign travel as well. Taken with data concerning Yugoslav border crossings, however, the pattern and its implications for an evolving Yugoslav elite attitude toward exit and open borders become quite striking indeed.

In 1950, the first year for which there are data, 41,000 foreign tourists visited Yugoslavia and spent a total of 179 thousand nights there (see Table 4.2). This amounted to only 1.7 percent of all Yugoslav tourism and 2.1 percent of the nights spent in tourist accommodations. By 1963, 1,755,000 foreign tourists spending 7.649 million nights visited Yugoslavia annually and foreign tourism had come to constitute 29.3 percent of all Yugoslav tourism (with 18 percent of nights spent in tourism). By 1973, 6,149 million foreign tourists visited Yugoslavia—43 percent of the total—and spent 32.04 million nights (half of all tourist nights) visiting Yugoslavia. These figures then remain relatively constant in the decade 1973-1983.

The number of foreigners crossing the Yugoslav borders grows in a parallel way (see Table 4.3). According to data from the Yugoslav Secretariat for Internal Affairs (SUP), slightly more than a million foreigners crossed the Yugoslav border in 1960. That number had increased to more than 8.3 million by 1965, and to approximately 30 million in 1970. It then drops off sharply in 1971 and gradually increases through the 1970s, although the 1975 and 1976 figures are well short of the 1969-1970 ones.

The trends reflecting the increased openness of the Yugoslav border

TABLE 4.2
Tourism in Yugoslavia, 1950-1983 (In thousands)

Year	Tourists	Of which Foreign	Tourist "Nights"	Of which Foreign
1950	2,361	41	8,819	179
1953	3,179	245	8,140	855
1963	5,999	1,755	25,878	7,649
1973	14,297	6,149	64,052	32,037
1977	16,587	5,621	73,488	29,026
1978	18,294	6,385	83,546	34,866
1979	17,645	5,966	81,499	33,482
1980	18,089	6,410	87,106	36,978
1981	18,741	6,616	90,508	39,695
1982	18,472	5,955	88,814	35,580
1983	18,790	5,947	90,649	35,355

SOURCES: *Statisticki godisnjak Jugoslavije*, 1982, p. 95; 1984, p. 344. Savezni zavod za statistiku, *Indeks*, No. 4 (April 1983), pp. 70-71.

TABLE 4.3
Yugoslav Border Crossings, 1960-1976 (In thousands)

Year	Foreigners Crossing Yugoslav Borders	Yugoslavs Crossing Yugoslav Borders
1960	1,157	191
1961	1,387	255
1962	1,765	292
1963	2,561	299
1964	3,961	449
1965	8,316	1,284
1966	16,820	3,360
1967	22,351	6,961
1968	23,206	8,107
1969	30,227	10,692
1970	29,393	14,474
1971	21,752	11,759
1972	21,593	12,476
1973	23,800	14,003
1974	20,586	13,758
1975	24,149	13,806
1976	25,909	16,013

SOURCE: Micovic [1977], p. 115. (He, in turn, reports the Yugoslav SUP as his source.)

which most bespoke a shift in Yugoslav regime-society relations, however, are those involving *Yugoslav* crossings of the Yugoslav border. In 1960 there were slightly less than 200,000 border crossings by Yugoslavs (16.5 percent of the number of foreign border crossings into Yugoslavia) annually. By 1965, 1,284 million border crossings by Yugoslavs were noted by the Yugoslav authorities. This number had increased to 14,474 million Yugoslav crossings of the Yugoslav borders annually by 1970. The 14-million figure was approximately half the number of foreigners crossing the Yugoslav border annually. (The Yugoslav population in the 1971 census was 20.5 million.) Just as in the case of foreign border crossings into Yugoslavia, there is a sharp drop in the number of Yugoslavs leaving the country between 1970 and 1971, though by 1976 the figures for Yugoslav departures had exceeded the figures for 1970.

Overall, however, the pattern is clear in both instances: the gradual political relaxation, the economic reforms, the liberalization of the passport service—combined with European prosperity—produced a radical change in the permeability of the Yugoslav borders. As a result, what at the beginning of the decade was a relative rarity had become by 1970 an absolutely ordinary event. In 1960 on the average about 500 Yugoslavs crossed Yugoslavia's border somewhere daily; by 1970 roughly 40,000 Yugoslavs were crossing Yugoslavia's borders every day. It was in that changed political context that Yugoslav workers found it possible to respond to the economic pull of jobs and higher wages in Western Europe.

And go, they did. (The demand for Yugoslav workers in Germany was increased by the East German construction of the Berlin Wall in 1960.) The trickle of the 1950s became by the mid-1960s a rivulet: from roughly 18,000 at work in Europe in 1960, the number of Yugoslav workers abroad increased to approximately 28,000 in 1961, 42,000 in 1962, 80,000 in 1964, 130,000 in 1965 (see Table 4.4). With the economic reforms, the rivulet became a flood—a flood which abated only with the stagflation and recession that followed the 1973 jump in global oil prices. Exactly how many were abroad in various years after 1965 is difficult to report; estimates vary considerably. The Yugoslav figures are consistently lower than are the data of the recipient countries, although the gap has generally narrowed over time. (This reflects the growing tendency for Yugoslav migrants to go abroad under Federal Employment Bureau auspices rather than privately qua tourist.) At the onset of the reforms in 1965, there were approximately 130,000 Yugoslavs working in Europe. By 1967 that number had almost doubled to 220,000 despite the economic slowdown in West Germany. That number in turn had trebled by 1971. Two years later, in 1973, what may have been the peak figure of 860,000 was reached; in 1974 and 1975 the recession in Europe produced a decrease in the number of Yugoslavs in Western Europe. Whereas in 1973 there were 860,000, by 1974 that number had decreased to 800,000, to 770,000 in 1975 and to 725,000 in 1976, 695,000 in 1978 and 625,000 in 1981. (It remains to be seen, of course, whether the 1973 figures for the workers themselves will ever be reattained.)

These figures, moreover, do not include Yugoslavs working outside Eu-

TABLE 4.4
Number of Yugoslav Workers in Western Europe, 1960-1979

Year	Yugoslav Workers in Europe	Year	Yugoslav Workers in Europe	Year	Yugoslav Workers in Europe
1960	18,000	1967	220,000	1974	810,000
1961	28,000	1968	260,000	1975	770,000
1962	42,000	1969	430,000	1976	725,000
1963	80,000	1970	600,000	1977	695,000
1964	105,000	1971	680,000	1978	685,000
1965	130,000	1972	770,000	1979	680,000
1966	190,000	1973	860,000		

SOURCES: For 1962-1976, Baucic [1979]; for 1977-1979, Nejasmic [1981], p. 16.

rope in Australia, Canada, the United States, and elsewhere, nor do they include family members accompanying the workers to Europe or elsewhere. The ratio of nonworking family members to workers has not been constant. In the late 1960s few dependents accompanied the Yugoslav worker to Europe; in the recessionary 1970s by contrast a much larger number of nonworking Yugoslavs joined the working member or members of the family abroad (see below). The 1971 and 1981 Yugoslav censuses—both of which underestimate the number of Yugoslavs abroad—place, respectively, 91,818 and 249,896 nonworking members of families abroad. (Recipient country figures probably constitute better estimates. Grecic [1975, p. 230] notes that there is a gap of 152,000 between the expected and actual totals in the 1971 census. Presumably virtually all of the unaccounted for were abroad.) If the censuses have the proportions of working and nonworking Yugoslavs abroad correct, then the total number of Yugoslavs abroad did not decrease but actually increased during the decade 1971-1981. The 1971 census counted 671,908 workers abroad or a total of approximately 763,000 Yugoslav workers and their families. The 1981 census counts 625,000 workers abroad or a total of approximately 875,000 workers and their families. Baucic's 1975 and 1979 estimates are more plausible. Throughout the 1970s there were roughly 200,000 Yugoslav workers and 100,000 dependents outside Europe. Baucic estimates the total number of Yugoslavs abroad for 1975 [interview] and for Europe for 1979 [1979, p. 17] at 1.340 million and 1.080 million (including 650,000 workers) respectively. Both figures imply that an estimate for the mid-1970s and the outset of the 1980s of 1,300,000 as the number of Yugoslavs abroad would not likely be far off.

By way of comparison, the population of the six republics in the 1971 and 1981 censuses are shown in Table 4.5. In brief, the number, of Yugoslav workers in Europe (i.e., not including workers outside Europe or nonworking relatives of Yugoslavs working abroad) exceeded the population of Montenegro at the time of either the 1971 or 1981 census. The total number of Yugoslavs abroad in the 1970s at any one time was roughly the same as that of the population of Kosovo during the 1970s and roughly two-thirds the population of Slovenia, Macedonia or Vojvodina. If, in addition, we take into account not only those who are abroad at any given moment and those who have returned, the total number becomes even larger. Nejasmic [1981, p. 16] estimates that in the period between 1968 and 1979, 657,000 Yugoslav workers returned from Europe and 1,157,000 went to Europe. Since there were already 220,000 Yugoslav workers in Europe at the end of 1967, this would imply that the total number of Yugoslavs and their families who had gone abroad to work "temporarily" is quite close to and may even exceed the population of Slovenia, Macedonia, or Vojvodina. Yugoslavs are engaging only in slight hyperbole when they term the Yugoslav migrant

TABLE 4.5
Yugoslav Population by Republic, 1971 and 1981

Republic	1971	1981
Bosnia-Hercegovina	3,746,111	4,124,008
Croatia	4,426,221	4,601,469
Macedonia	1,647,308	1,912,257
Montenegro	529,604	584,310
Slovenia	1,727,137	1,891,864
SR Serbia		
Serbia proper	5,250,365	5,694,464
Kosovo	1,243,693	1,584,441
Vojvodina	1,952,533	2,034,772
Total	20,522,972	22,427,585

SOURCE: *Statisticki bilten*, no. 1295 (1982).

workers and their families abroad "our seventh republic." Indeed, the notion that the Yugoslav workers abroad constitute a seventh republic conveys as well as one phrase could the sense that "Yugoslavia"—the political community of Yugoslav citizens who expect services and rights from, and render obligations to, a Yugoslav government—and the legally demarcated borders of Yugoslavia are not coextensive.

THE SEVENTH REPUBLIC: CHANGING DEMOGRAPHIC COMPOSITION

What then, is the seventh republic, this Yugoslav archipelago, the main islands of which are located in Western Europe but which extends to Australia? How does the seventh republic's demographic profile compare with that of the other six republics, and what trends are discernible over time? How do we explain the outmigration of Yugoslav workers?

The seventh republic, naturally enough, is drawn from the other six republics. In the 1960s, the migration was a disproportionately Croatian affair. For that period we have data on the year-by-year migration pattern by republic, and as Table 4.6 reveals, Bakaric was clearly correct when he characterized the first years of the outflow as largely a Croatian phenomenon.

By the time of the 1971 census about half again as many persons from Croatia were abroad (33.4 percent) as one would expect by simply extrapolating from the 1971 census. Among the other republics only Bosnia-Hercegovina (20.4 percent) was represented abroad by a larger proportion of the total than a simple extrapolation would predict. (Using recipient country totals rather than the 1971 census as a basis for computations, Macedonia with 9.1 percent of the workers abroad would also be overrepresented.) The

TABLE 4.6
Proportion of Yugoslavs Going Abroad Annually by Republic (In percentages)

Republic	1960	1961	1962	1963	1964	1965	1966
Bosnia-Hercegovina	8.6	15.2	14.7	16.2	17.5	14.6	13.3
Croatia	56.0	51.2	56.0	50.6	39.2	36.3	39.9
Macedonia	7.8	5.9	4.8	4.6	6.4	7.2	6.8
Montenegro	0.8	0.4	0.6	0.6	0.5	0.7	0.7
Slovenia	16.2	15.6	11.7	9.6	12.2	13.2	12.7
Serbia proper	7.1	8.5	8.4	13.3	17.6	19.3	17.4
Kosovo	0.4	0.3	0.3	0.3	0.3	0.6	0.5
Vojvodina	3.1	2.9	3.5	4.8	6.3	8.1	8.7
Total %	100	100	100	100	100	100	100
YUGOSLAVS ABROAD	15,342	4,288	8,131	8,682	10,204	20,373	25,855

Republic	1967	1968	1969	1970	1971*	Unkn.	Total
Bosnia-Hercegovina	14.9	16.7	19.1	21.6	28.3	17.8	20.4
Croatia	40.2	42.4	37.8	28.7	24.0	31.1	33.4
Macedonia	8.2	6.9	7.3	9.1	8.7	7.5	8.1
Montenegro	1.0	1.5	1.5	1.3	1.0	1.1	1.2
Slovenia	10.0	9.4	7.2	5.1	4.5	10.3	7.2
Serbia proper	16.8	12.7	13.5	19.5	19.9	17.2	17.1
Kosovo	0.6	1.5	2.9	4.7	5.9	6.6	3.6
Vojvodina	8.2	8.9	10.7	10.0	7.7	8.4	9.0
Total %	100	100	100	100	100	100	100
YUGOSLAVS ABROAD	26,920	57,238	123,639	239,779	116,724	14,733	671,908

SOURCE: Savezni zavod za statistiku, "Lica na privremenom radu u inostranstvu," *Statisticki Bilten*, No. 679 (1971), p. 9. For the same computation, see Baucic [1973], p. 43.
*January to March 1971.

other republics either had a number abroad that approximated their proportion in the Yugoslav population—Slovenia, Vojvodina, Macedonia (with the qualification noted above); or, most notably with regard to Serbia proper (17.1 percent instead of 25.6 percent), Kosovo (3.6 percent rather than 6.1 percent), and Montenegro (1.2 percent in comparison with 2.6 percent), were considerably lower (see Table 4.7).

Similarly, when the numbers abroad are computed in terms of nationality declared in the 1971 census, it turns out that slightly more than one-fifth (22.2 percent) of the country identified themselves as Croat in the 1971 census; slightly less than two-fifths (39 percent) of those abroad were Croat (see Table 4.8). Moreover, a comparison of the ethnic background of the migrants from Bosnia-Hercegovina furthers the sense that initially the migration was disproportionately a Croatian affair. According to the 1971 census,

TABLE 4.7
Yugoslavs Abroad by Republic, 1971 and 1981 (In percentages)

Republic	1971		1981	
	% of Total Yugoslav Population	% of Republic's Workers Abroad	% of Total Yugoslav Population	% of Republic's Workers Abroad
Bosnia-Hercegovina	18.3	· 20.4	18.4	21.4
Croatia	21.6	33.4	20.5	24.3
Macedonia	8.0	8.1	8.5	9.3
Montenegro	2.6	1.2	2.6	1.6
Slovenia	8.4	7.2	8.4	6.7
SR Serbia				
Serbia proper	25.6	17.1	25.4	24.5 ·
Kosovo	6.1	3.6	7.1	4.6
Vojvodina	9.5	9.0	9.1	7.7
	100.1	100.0	100.0	100.1

NOTE: Percentages exceed 100 because of rounding.
SOURCE: Baucic [1982], p. 324.

TABLE 4.8
Workers Abroad by Nationality, 1971

Nationality	% Abroad	% Total Yugoslavs
Albanian	5.2	6.4
Croatian	39.0	22.2
Hungarian	2.9	2.3
Mecedonian	5.7 (6.4)	5.9
Montenegrin	.8	2.5
"Muslim"	6.0	8.5
Serb	28.5	39.9
Slovene	7.0	7.8
Others	4.9	6.5
Total¹	100.0	100.0

SOURCE: Derived from Baucic, [1973], p. 83. See also *NIN*, No. 1149, January 14, 1973, pp. 31-32.

42.4 percent of the migrants from Bosnia-Hercegovina were Croat; only one-fifth (20.6 percent) of the republic was Croat [Baucic, 1973, p. 84].

However, Table 4.9 (based on data from the 1971 and 1981 censuses) reveals the extent to which what was originally a phenomenon restricted to Croatia and more generally to the northern republics (Croatia, Bosnia-Hercegovina, Vojvodina, and Slovenia) has become all-Yugoslav in scope. The relative role of the developed regions—Croatia, Vojvodina, and Slovenia—has clearly decreased over time. Correspondingly, the role of Serbia proper,

TABLE 4.9
Number of Workers Abroad by Republic: 1971 and 1981 Compared

Republic	1971	1981	1981 as Proportion of 1971
Bosnia-Hercegovina	137,351	133,902	97.5
Croatia	224,722	151,619	67.5
Macedonia	54,433	57,962	106.5
Montenegro	7,829	9,781	124.9
Slovenia	48,086	41,826	86.9
SR Serbia			
Serbia proper	114,581	152,932	133.5
Kosovo	24,361	28,965	118.9
Vojvodina	60,545	48,078	79.4
Total	671,908	625,065	93.0

SOURCE: Baucic [1982], p. 324.

Montenegro, Macedonia, and Kosovo has grown steadily, while Bosnia-Hercegovina has remained overrepresented in the migration, even though it experienced a slight decline in absolute numbers between 1971 and 1981. It is very likely that in 1971, when Croatian nationalists were most vociferously protesting the disproportional contributions the Croatian workers abroad were making to Yugoslavia's balance of payments through their remittances, the role of Croatia and of Croats in the migration was already diminishing. Certainly, by the end of the 1970s the number of Croatian workers temporarily abroad had decreased sharply: only two-thirds as many Croatian workers are identified as being abroad in 1981 as in 1971.

In 1961 were one to meet a Yugoslav in the seventh republic—or less metaphorically in a railroad station in Munich or Vienna—he or she would have very likely been a Croat from Croatia. Croats and Croatians were similarly overrepresented in the migration in 1971. In the 1981 census (see Table 4.9), however, Croatians were only slightly overrepresented among the Yugoslavs classified as temporarily abroad, and the great increases in the numbers—though the increases were not sufficient to result in these republics being overrepresented in the migration—were from Serbia proper, Montenegro, and Kosovo.

As in Yugoslavia, however, the distribution of persons by republic (and by implication by nationality) in the various islands of the archipelago that make up the seventh republic varies considerably. The 1971 census figures reveal that the republics of Bosnia-Hercegovina and Croatia were particularly well represented in Germany. A majority of the Yugoslavs in France in 1971 were from Serbia proper (although there were twice as many from Serbia in Germany as in France), while in Austria one found large proportions from the Republic of Serbia (Serbia proper, Kosovo, and Vojvodina). Outside Europe, one finds a large concentration in the United States of the few Montenegrins who were abroad (10.4 percent of the total Yugoslav workers in the U.S. and 32 percent of all Montenegrins abroad); and there is an unusually large concentration from Macedonia in the total number of Yugoslav workers in Australia [Baucic, 1973].

Sex distribution among Yugoslavs abroad almost exactly parallels that of the work force in Yugoslavia. According to the 1971 census, slightly more than 31 percent of those working abroad in 1971 were women; slightly less than 32 percent of the work force in 1971 were women. Yugoslav women abroad, however, come disproportionately from republics where women make up a sizable fraction of the work force in that republic and from areas close to the Austrian and Italian borders. Disproportionately fewer women come from those areas most dominated by traditional notions about women—Muslim Bosnia-Hercegovina, Montenegro, Macedonia, and most notably, Kosovo. Few people from Kosovo had migrated abroad to work at the time of the 1971 census. Of them, 19 out of 20 were men, a ratio far exceeding that found in Kosovo itself, where 82.1 percent of the work force are men [*Statisticki godisnjak Jugoslavije*, 1972; Baucic, 1973].

Yugoslav women who go abroad are younger than the men. As a result, a composite age profile is somewhat misleading. The average age of men working abroad appears to be greater than Yugoslavs widely believe. Moreover, some aging of the work force abroad seems to have taken place in the 1970s since fewer Yugoslavs were going abroad to work in these years, and a large fraction of those with jobs in Western Europe were presumably keeping them rather than returning home. This at least is the finding of Ivica Nejasmic based on a 1977 survey of 822 returning migrants in Bosnia-Hercegovina, Croatia, and Serbia (see Table 4.10).

Finally, the work skills of those who go abroad vary in significant ways from the profile of the Yugoslav domestic work force, and it is easy to become confused on this score. Great credence has been attached in the Yugoslav media to the view that Yugoslav workers in Western Europe, in sharp contrast to the Italian, Spanish, Portuguese, and Greek workers, tend to be skilled rather than unskilled. In fact, however, skilled workers go abroad in proportions comparable to their numbers in the Yugoslav work force. Disproportionately, it is the unskilled and semiskilled who go abroad. These are overwhelmingly peasants.

Interestingly, though, it is rarely Yugoslavs—peasants or otherwise—with virtually no education who migrate; 24 percent of the Yugoslav population in the 1971 census had a third-grade education or less, but only 10 percent of the migrants had so little education. At the other end of the educational scale, likewise, Yugoslavs are less likely to go abroad. Dispropor-

TABLE 4.10

Trends in the Age Structure of Yugoslav Migrant
Workers, 1971-1977 (In percentages)

Age	1971 Census	1977 Survey
Under 30	52.5%	37.7%
30-50	43.3%	55.9%
Over 50	3.4%	6.4%
Unknown	0.8%	—
Total	100.0%	100.0%

SOURCES: *Statisticki Bilten*, No. 679 (1971), p. 10; Nejasmic [1981], p. 25.

NOTE: The aging generalization needs to be treated with
some caution pending the full figures from the 1981 census.

tionately fewer Yugoslavs who had completed high school (*gimnazija*),
school for middle-level industrial specialists, or who had university or other
post-secondary education migrated. Rather it was largely those with four or
more years of elementary school, or who had attended a school for qualified
or very qualified workers who went abroad.

Moreover, as Table 4.11 prefigures, of those whom the Yugoslav Statistical Office classifies as workers—roughly two-fifths of the total—a rather
large number are skilled workers. In the 1971 census, the fraction of non-
skilled and semiskilled workers abroad, even among ''workers'' narrowly
defined, [*Statisticki bilten*, 1971, No. 679, p. 12] was somewhat higher
than the national average (see Table 4.12). Still, some 45 percent of those
who were abroad in 1971 were skilled or highly skilled workers, as opposed
to only 32 percent of the Yugoslav cohort of ''workers.'' In brief, those who
are skilled—those with university training and/or office, clerical, or mana-
gerial skills—but who are not working class in the customary sense, or in
the meaning employed by the Yugoslav Statistical Office, remain in Yugoslavia. A large fraction of those who go abroad are not ''workers'' in the
sense employed by the Yugoslav Statistical Office, since those who work
with private means of production—generally peasants and others who are
self-employed—are not defined as ''workers.'' Especially in the 1960s and
early 1970s, the first job the Yugoslav peasant obtained after he or she left
the land was often in Munich. To Munich—or Frankfurt, or Vienna—he or
she went in search of any kind of job. (Subsequently, the first move was
more typically to Ljubljana or Zagreb.) The peasant abroad is joined by socialist Yugoslavia's skilled and unskilled proletariat; they—workers as defined by the Yugoslav Statistical Office—presumably had come to capitalist
Munich to seek higher wages.

TABLE 4.11
Yugoslav Workers: A Skills Profile, December 1970 (In percentages)

	Yugoslavia*	Croatia*	Croatian Workers Sample Abroad†	Men among Croatian Sample Abroad†
Unskilled	24.5	14.3	48.6	43.1
Semiskilled	12.7	16.2	9.8	11.0
Skilled	25.2	28.9	29.9	35.7
Highly skilled	6.6	8.8	3.3	4.3
Elementary School	7.9	4.0	2.7	1.5
High school	14.2	15.5	4.4	3.2
University and advanced schooling	8.9	12.2	1.3	1.1
Total	100.0	99.9	100.0	99.9

SOURCES: Baucic and Maravic [1971], p. 77.
*Computed from *Statisticki godisnjak Jugoslavije* 1972, pp. 93, 357.
†*Statisticki Bilten*, No. 679 (1971), p. 10.

TABLE 4.12
Education Achieved and Migration (In percentages)

Schooling Completed	Yugoslavia	Yugoslavs Working Abroad	
		1971	1977
Under 3 years	24.3	10.1	6.8
4-7 years	42.5	46.1	40.9
Elementary school	14.6	19.8	26.1
School for qualified or very qualified workers	9.0	16.6	17.8
Gimnazia	2.0	1.2	1.1
Technical school for middle-level experts	4.3	3.0	4.4
University or other post-secondary	2.9	1.5	1.7
Unknown	.4	1.7	1.2
Total	100.0	100.0	100.0

SOURCE: Nejasmic [1981], p. 20.

EXPLAINING THE OUTMIGRATION OF YUGOSLAV WORKERS

A standard complaint about social science research is that it reminds one of the old anecdote about the person who, having lost his contact lens in the plush carpet of the living room, searches for it in the bathroom where the light is better. Those who yield to the temptation, it is contended, focus on that which is most easily observed or quantified without regard for whether such matters are also the most important, causally. Such a temptation certainly exists with respect to explanations of the migration of Yugoslav workers abroad. There is, as we shall see, a ready sense in which unemployment in Yugoslavia and employment opportunities and higher wages in Western Europe drive the migration process. It cannot be emphasized too strongly, however, that pride of place in understanding the migration of Yugoslav workers abroad must be allotted to the political in an inventory of explanatory variables. It was a conscious attitude change by Yugoslav communist elites and the concomitant policy choices that flowed from these changes and resulted in Yugoslavia's opening to the world that produced the economic phenomenon of Yugoslav workers abroad. To explain why Yugoslavia is like Portugal, Spain, Turkey, and Greece is to understand first of all the ways Yugoslavia in the 1950s and 1960s became unlike Bulgaria, Romania, and Czechoslovakia. Given that attitude change, economic and other nonpolitical considerations must be added to the policy choices of Yugoslav and other decisionmakers to explain who, among the Yugoslavs, migrates where and the changes in the propensity to migrate on the part of various Yugoslavs.

Similarly, if that attitude were reversed, Yugoslavia could once again be more appropriately classed with patterns typically associated with East European communist states rather than with southern European states. As we have seen, high politics mattered in 1965-1966: had not Rankovic been ousted, the implementation of the reforms and the subsequent opening of the borders would presumably have been modest in scope. The connections which Rankovic's police had with their Soviet counterparts were ostensibly a major element in his political demise, and it is possible that some future major shift in the Yugoslav leadership might again occur which would indirectly produce a significant change in migration behavior. One can say with near certainty that in 1972-1973 the extent and direction of Yugoslavia's general linkages with the international environment were a matter of central importance in the country's high politics. Furthermore, in the aftermath of Tito's well-known "Letter," the purge of Marko Nikezic (the Serbian republic party leader), and the removal of Stane Kavcic (then Slovenian Prime Minister)—all during the fall of 1972—there seemed for a while a genuine possibility that internal "consolidation" would imply the extensive use of administrative measures to restrict the outflow of Yugoslavs wishing to leave the country.

What resulted instead was a series of more limited measures. Legislation was passed in 1973 making it illegal to work abroad prior to having completed one's military tour of duty; without ensuring the education of children left behind; or if an equivalent job existed in Yugoslavia. In addition, those who were officers in the reserve were restricted from working abroad. Steps were also taken to ensure that Yugoslavs abroad who were engaged in rendering services to Yugoslavs—*not* the Yugoslav workers themselves—working abroad had an appropriately high level of political consciousness.

A decade later it was virtually impossible to assess the impact of these measures on the Yugoslav propensity to migrate. The year 1973 will be better remembered as the year of the oil shock. In the decade following, the absence of jobs in Europe dominated the overall situation; it remains to be seen whether in the coming years the numbers, the mix of Yugoslavs working abroad, or the duration of their stay will be altered by the legal context provided by the new federal laws and interrepublic agreements.

In a political setting in which the openness of the country's borders is a central claim to Yugoslavia's distinctiveness—in which, in Marxist terms, the political superstructure allows processes in the base to operate—it is an intriguing exercise to identify the other elements that influence the magnitude and composition of the migration. In so doing, one is struck immediately by the role of events exogenous to Yugoslavia and by the extent to which ostensibly internal variables—level of development, informal communications networks, and individual preference patterns—have a strong international and extra-Yugoslav component.

The External Environment

Thus, in explaining the overall volume of the outflow, the general economic situation in Europe must be considered an integral part of an explanation of Yugoslav migration rates. Of the European states, Germany is the most important. There is an impressive relationship between the demand for foreign workers in Germany and the outmigration of Yugoslav workers. One factor, for instance, in explaining the outmigration of Yugoslav workers in the early 1960s was the construction of the Berlin Wall which removed the possibility that East Germans could satisfy the intensive demand for labor in West Germany. Moreover, the linkage between slowdowns in the German economy and the Yugoslav external migration rate is impressively straightforward. From 1966 to 1968, the German economy was in a slump, and the number of Yugoslavs remained essentially constant in Germany and in Europe as a whole. There were 96,000 Yugoslav workers in Germany in 1966; 97,725 in 1967; 99,600 in 1968; and 226,290 in 1969. For Europe as a whole the best estimates for 1966, 1967, and 1968 are 190,000, 220,000, and 260,000 respectively, and 430,000 for 1969 [Baucic, 1979, p. 6].

The Yugoslav-supported Arab oil embargo and the subsequent stagflationary recession in Western Europe had an even more dramatic impact on both the number of Yugoslavs going abroad in various years and on the total number of Yugoslavs in Germany in particular, and in Western Europe more generally. Table 4.13 shows the number of Yugoslav workers who went

TABLE 4.13
Changes in Yugoslav Migration Flows to Western Europe in the 1970s

Year	Departees Annually	Returnees Annually	Yugoslav Workers in Germany*	Yugoslav Workers in Europe
1970	240,000	70,00	389,953	600,000
1971	145,000	65,000	469,173	680,000
1972	145,000	55,000	471,892	770,000
1973	115,000	25,000	535,000	860,000
1974	30,000	80,000	473,203	810,000
1975	30,000	70,000	418,745	770,000
1976	25,000	70,000	390,079	725,000
1977	30,000	60,000	375,200	695,000
1978	32,000	42,000	369,506	685,000
1979	35,000	40,000	—	680,000

SOURCES: Nejasmic [1981], p. 16, for columns 1, 2, and 4.
*Baucic [1979], p. 6, citing official German sources.

abroad each year, the number who returned in the course of a given year, along with the total number of Yugoslavs working in Germany and Western Europe. As Table 4.14 reveals, surprisingly, during the 1970s the number returning to Yugoslavia per year did not vary drastically. Rather, the number of departures from Yugoslavia decreased abruptly with the downturn in the European economy.

The impression that the Yugoslav economy is inextricably linked to the European market for labor is further enhanced when we focus not merely on the flows of Yugoslav workers but consider the movements of their families as well. As jobs dried up in Western Europe, fewer Yugoslav workers (and their Turkish and Greek counterparts) went abroad. As we have seen, the total number of Yugoslav workers in Europe decreased substantially in the aftermath of the 1973 jump in world oil prices and the subsequent stagflation in the industrialized world. There were a total of 8.2 million *gastarbeiter* in Europe in 1973 and only 6.5 million in 1978. The number of Yugoslav workers decreased by approximately 165,000 (from 860,000 to 685,000) between those dates. Simultaneously, however, the number of family members in Western Europe increased substantially—especially, the evidence suggests, in the immediate aftermath of the oil shock (1974-1975). Whereas there were roughly 5 million members of the families of the *gastarbeiter* in Europe in 1973, that number had increased to 6.2 million by 1978. The Yugoslav change was even more dramatic, going from 250,000 in 1973 to 385,000 by 1978 [Baucic, 1979, p. 13].

The result was a kind of curious equilibrium. Those Yugoslavs with steady jobs stayed in Western Europe. Few Yugoslav workers have gone to Europe since 1973. This produced a stabilization in the Yugoslav migrant worker population in Western Europe. As in the case of buildings constructed in wartime Washington, "temporary" turns out to be a long time: by the fall of 1977, 62 percent of all Yugoslav citizens in Germany had been there for six or more years and 71.2 percent of those Yugoslavs age six or over [*Statistisches Bundesant* in Wiesbaden as cited by Baucic, 1979, p. 16]. During the 1970s, the nonworking members of the families of those Yugoslavs with secure jobs increasingly joined their spouses in Western Europe. (Almost 88 percent of those abroad according to the 1971 census were workers; the 1981 census counts 71 percent of those Yugoslavs abroad as workers and the remainder as family members [*Statisticki godisnjak Jugoslavije*, 1984, p. 443].) As a result, the export of unemployment in the 1970s from Western Europe in the Yugoslav case was almost exactly offset by the Yugoslav export of its social welfare burden to Western Europe. The net change in the number of Yugoslavs in Western Europe, consequently, during the tumultuous five years from 1973 to 1978 was only 30,000, out of slightly more than a million Yugoslavs in Western Europe—despite the fact that the number of Yugoslav workers in Europe decreased by almost one-fifth (165,000).

Moreover, the notion that factors exogenous to Yugoslavia are an essential part of an explanation for Yugoslav migration flows ought not be restricted to a reified and abstract international market. Attention is due the conscious policies of major corporate actors external to Yugoslavia that may directly or indirectly alter Yugoslav migration flows. Of these, the major West European states, by their social policies, are key, but they also include the great powers, international organizations, and the permanent Yugoslav political emigration.

Thus, the Germans (and Austrians, Swedes, Swiss, French) can and do regulate the conditions under which Yugoslavs and other migrant workers enter and work in their country. It is they who can counter the lost human capital argument and can provide (or not provide) social welfare benefits to migrant workers and their families. To give but one obvious example, the number and composition of the Yugoslavs in West Germany would alter fundamentally were child supplements not provided the migrant workers. (For a candid recognition that this is so, see *NIN*, May 10, 1981, p. 23.)

The governments of Western Europe affect Yugoslav migration rates when they act collectively as well. After all, it has been rightly remarked that "the signing of the Rome Agreement in 1957 and the founding of the European Economic Community represented the most significant step [in the liberalization of migration flows among the European States]. And if the creation of the EEC included in the integration process only six West European countries, it constituted the beginning of an integrated labor market inasmuch as the work force of countries which were not members of the Community (Spain, Portugal, Greece, Turkey, and Yugoslavia) were included" in it [Svetislav Polovina, *Nase teme*, December 1969, pp. 1949-50]. Subsequent decisions, likewise, including the conditions under which various southern European states join the Community could also have had profound effects on the migration patterns of the nonmember states. For Yugoslavia particularly, the 1980 trade agreement between Yugoslavia and the EEC is especially important since it accords the Yugoslavs the same treatment as workers from North Africa and other Mediterranean states.

Other possible relevant exogenous actors are the great powers and the Yugoslav political emigration. The connection between the superpowers and their interactions and migration patterns may seem, initially, rather tenuous. Nevertheless, the improvement in Soviet- American relations between 1972 and 1975 seems to have furthered the general sense among the Yugoslav elite of the importance of going it alone. This in turn seems to have been at the heart of the 1973 legislation designed specifically to prevent those who had not satisfied their military obligation from going abroad to work. Similarly, direct criticisms by Soviet commentators of the policy of allowing workers abroad, or even more broad critiques of the general Yugoslav orientation, may have had a bearing on the policies adopted with a view to regulating the outflow of workers. At a time (1973) when Belgrade was clearly sensitive to Soviet remarks, observations in the Soviet press—written while the Yugoslavs were adopting a series of measures to regulate the outflow of workers—were surely targeted at Yugoslavia. One Soviet article published in March 1973 faulted the views of "some persons in the West" who accentuate the positive about the internal consequences of a mass migration policy. It claimed that "the FRG . . . completely avoids any investment whatsoever in infrastructure (kindergartens, hospitals, schools)"; that "the facts reveal a slowing of economic growth in a number of countries exporting the main productive force—workers"; "that the emptying and degradation of entire geographic regions . . . [and] a worsening of the age structure of the population is taking place" [Okun, 1973, pp. 137-138]. Such assertions may find a distinct resonance in Yugoslavia. That having been said, it should also be borne in mind that for every Yugoslav impressed by arguments stemming from Soviet sources there is another disposed to reject a proposal that smacks of the Soviet model. Consequently, Soviet willingness—or, as it turned out in practice, lack thereof—to deliver the $1.3 billion in credits promised in 1973 was much more likely to have had an impact on the marginal propensity of Yugoslavs to migrate than were statements appearing in the Soviet press.

The same could also be said for the United States and the International

Bank for Reconstruction and Development—the U.S. by reducing the risks for private American investment in Yugoslavia; the IBRD by its policy of encouraging infrastructural development in Yugoslavia and by its cultivation of Adriatic development schemes; and, more recently, the development of the south.

Similarly, the political emigration has to be factored in some way. Its existence surely had a deterrent effect on the critical decision to open the borders, and it has been a source of concern to the Yugoslav authorities over the years, especially immediately after the Croatian events of 1971 and the Kosovo riots a decade later. Were it demonstrated that the political emigration had a substantial impact on attitudes of Yugoslav workers abroad, this would almost certainly have an impact on Yugoslav migration policies: the already-considerable efforts of the government to inform and shape the opinions of the Yugoslav workers abroad would be augmented by administrative measures to affect the number and political attitudes of those allowed to go abroad. (On the efforts to mobilize the opinion of those abroad, see below, pp. 118-122.)

INTERNATIONAL-NATIONAL LINKAGES AND YUGOSLAV MIGRATORY FLOWS

Similarly, there are clear linkages between the international environment and important putatively "internal" explanations of Yugoslav migration rates. Consider, for instance, the link between level of development and migration. One of the major trends in postwar demographic patterns in Yugoslavia has been a movement away from the land. The agricultural population of Yugoslavia constituted roughly two-thirds (67.2 percent) of the Yugoslav population in 1948. By the 1971 census, it was less than two-fifths (38.2 percent) and by the 1981 census, it was about one-fifth. (The 1984 *Yugoslav Statistical Yearbook* reports 19.9 percent, excluding persons abroad; by that criterion the 1971 figure would be 36.6 percent) [*Statisticki godisnjak Jugoslavije*, 1976, p. 103; 1984, p. 114]. While the total number employed in the sense used by the Yugoslav Statistical Office has increased substantially and steadily throughout the post-World War II period (see Table 4.14), the industrial and tertiary sectors—as Yugoslav observers have widely recognized—have not been able to absorb the growing pool of potential workers. As the country has industrialized, migration abroad has provided a safety valve for the dramatic shifts in population away from the villages.

Indeed, given the openness of Yugoslavia's borders to the outmigration of labor, there is a temptation to view Yugoslav migration simply as part of an overall market for labor—as one facet of an equilibrium mechanism for la-

TABLE 4.14
Employment and Unemployment in Yugoslavia, 1952-1984 (In thousands)

Year	Employed in Social Sector	Unemployed	Year	Employed in Social Sector	Unemployed
1952	1,734	45	1980	5,798	785
1962	3,318	237	1981	5,966	809
1972	4,210	315	1982	6,104	862
1978	5,383	735	1983	6,223	910
1979	5,615	762	1984	6,355	975

SOURCES: Savezni zavod za statistiku, *Indeks*, No. 10 (October 1983), p. 42; No. 7 (July 1985), p. 42.

bor, primarily in Europe. And in fact one Yugoslav scholar, Vladimir Grecic [1975, p. 154], has done precisely this: he has described the Yugoslav migration as simply one point along a regression line that summarizes an overall equation for Europe as a whole. In that equation, gross national product per capita and outmigration rates are inversely related, and demands for services in the European labor market call forth a response in labor supply. Using figures drawn from 1968-1970, Grecic calculates that a parsimonious depiction ($r = 0.82$, $r^2 = 0.67$) of European migration patterns is represented by the equation $Y = \$1,382.18 - 125.58X$ where Y equals gross national product per capita and X equals migration. Using that equation one finds (as the high r^2 suggests) an impressive goodness of fit between the expected and observed values for intra-European labor flows.

There are, however, at least two fundamental problems with Grecic's parsimonious model. In one respect, Grecic's analysis was time bound in its assumptions about the international economy. Simply put, it implied full employment in Europe and presumed that there indeed existed a substantial demand for labor in Western Europe. As we have seen, labor flows from Yugoslavia can be strongly and adversely affected by the state of the economies of Western Europe. In that respect, Grecic's model was a partial one, relevant only for full employment conditions.

A problem of a different sort with Grecic's model is that it implies that all parts of Yugoslavia are equally integrated into the international economy. His model correctly anticipates that Yugoslavia would be a country of outmigration but tells us little about where the workers who left Yugoslavia in the 1960s and early 1970s came from. An inverse relationship between income per capita and migration could be detected at the nation-state level. At the republic level, the relationship circa 1970 was, if anything, the reverse. For the 1960s and early 1970s, *low* GNP per capita at the republic level was largely associated with *low* migration. Croatia and Slovenia by contrast

96

were among the leading sources of workers abroad. (Note though that it was Croatia and not Slovenia that headed the list.) Within republics, low GNP per capita per commune and high migration were characteristic of the more northern republics, but not of the Yugoslav south.

The reason, I suspect, is an important one: by the 1970s some parts of Yugoslavia were highly integrated into an overall European system while other areas were barely integrated in the Yugoslav market, much less the European market. Thus the Slovene sociologist, Veljko Rus [1972, p. 14] could write apropos of migration and the more developed regions of Yugoslavia that "Emigration and repatriation of the labor force is a form of very direct and very successful inclusion of national communities in a wider social space" and that "one of the general characteristics of an open system is that its parts or subsystems can be more intensively included in some processes or system outside Yugoslavia than within Yugoslavia."

Two consequences followed for understanding the migration flow. One was that, especially at the outset of the mass migration, there was an important difference between those areas where migration was a well-established alternative (e.g., the coastal and mountain regions of Croatia and Macedonia) before World War II or even World War I and elsewhere. "It is understandable that it will be easier to reach a decision to emigrate for a person whose father or grandfather has worked in some foreign country" [Baucic, 1970, p. 70]. Moreover, there might well be a relative or close friend living abroad who could facilitate a move (providing temporary quarters, making inquiries about jobs, etc.). Once these linkages had been reestablished, persons continued to gravitate in directions where relatives, friends, and, as the process burgeoned, friends of friends resided. In general, moreover, communication patterns and personal ties went a long way toward explaining where Yugoslavs went abroad to work. Cultural and historical reasons as well as economics must be considered in explaining why a disproportionately large number of Serbs went to France (they had relatives there from the interwar period, and they were fearful of *Ustasa* terrorism in Germany and had residual anti-German feelings); why the few Montenegrins who migrated in the 1960s and early 1970s disproportionately went to the United States; and why Macedonians went in large numbers to Australia. Similar explanations are relevant to understanding the extraordinary concentration of persons from single villages in particular West European locales. In some instances, in fact, the outmigration was so focused in the same region or city as to warrant Zivan Tanic's characterization of these concentrations as "micro-colonies" [1974, p. 88]. Thus, the small village of Grebenac in the Southern Banat had a population of 2,049 in the 1971 census. Of this total, nearly one-quarter (490) were working abroad. Of those, some 300 were employed in Salzburg. Similar concentrations from

the villages of Resavac and Svilajncan were to be found in Paris. For the
workers in Setonje, Innsbruck is just a long commute.

> Once a week there is direct communication from the village of Setonje
> to Innsbruck, Austria, or more exactly to the big factory in Innsbruck
> where almost the entire population of the village works. There, as in
> our village of Setonje, they are with one another constantly. There is
> almost no need to know the language. They are comfortable. They
> work harder than they would ever work at home. . . . They help very
> willingly in all the activities in the village. Now we will build a new
> clinic and they will invest the means. No one wants to stay there [in
> Innsbruck] longer and least of all forever. They don't want to take their
> children. So that the young will remain in the village, they buy them
> motorcycles and other diversionary things [Buric, 1973, p. 268].

The less developed republics and autonomous regions—and particularly
the less developed parts of those less developed republics and regions—by
contrast were far less tied to the international economic system. In 1970
there remained many areas where the village had only recently become
linked with the town; such areas were not yet plugged into an intra-Yugoslav
communications network and market, much less the more general European
market. Many places, especially in Kosovo and Montenegro, had not witnessed "the passing of traditional society"—to use Daniel Lerner's famous
phrase [1964]. They had not been sufficiently extricated from a patriarchal
and ordered society to be able to empathize in Lerner's sense—to imagine
themselves in some other context or occupying some other role. For an Albanian from Kosovo to go to work in Ljubljana in Slovenia, or even to Belgrade in Serbia proper, is to go abroad.

A model that explains which Yugoslavs go abroad needs to be one that
incorporates perceptions. Gross national product per capita at some low
level is a reflection of a nonmarket economy and a traditional society. Demands unperceived have no bearing on supply. The salience of political
boundaries may be reduced by the actions of central decision makers, but
cognitive boundaries—which themselves may be to a considerable extent a
function of modernization—may be more enduring. Market-oriented explanations, to be effective, must at a minimum be coupled with an attention to
existing formal and informal communication networks. The strident complaints of the Croatian nationalists in the early 1970s that an independent
Croatia, or a Croatia that was not subsidizing the less developed republics
of Yugoslavia, would rapidly achieve a level of development parallel to
Scandinavia illustrated, among other things, that for those in the north, the
relevant comparison was often extra-Yugoslav. Analogously, the intensity
with which Yugoslavs from the southeast, as Gary Bertsch [1971] has

shown, embrace egalitarian norms is a commentary on the perceived—and actual—asymmetries in the intra-Yugoslav standard of living. Given this frame of reference and level of aspiration, the Slovenes and Croatians who were dissatisfied with their economic lot went abroad, while those from the Yugoslav south, at least initially, did not.

Given the requisite awareness of options, the evidence available strongly suggests, nevertheless, that it is economics that drives Yugoslav migration to Western Europe and elsewhere. When we examine individual preference patterns, it becomes clear that the overwhelming number of respondents go abroad because they can earn more money there than at home. When asked why they went abroad, roughly two-thirds (64.3 percent) of a sample (N = 2311) from Bosnia-Hercegovina replied "higher wages" and one-quarter (24.5 percent) responded that they were unemployed. All other responses—family reasons, resolution of housing problems, adventure, schooling of children abroad, cooperation with foreign firms, specialization, others, and no response—received only 11.2 percent [Milojevic and Sultanovic, 1972]. In Baucic's and Maravic's study (based on interview data acquired from Croatians returning home during the Christmas–New Year vacation, 1970-1971) the "possibility of employment" found considerable response (36.3 percent), especially among women (61.2 percent) [1971, p. 80]. Nevertheless, for the total group the role of higher wages is as striking as in the Bosnia-Hercegovina study. The Croatian workers who had jobs in Yugoslavia went abroad in order to earn more money generally (9 percent) or for a specific purpose: to build a house (19.1 percent), to buy an apartment (6.3 percent), farm equipment (6.5 percent), or a private car (2.7 percent), or to open a business (6.2 percent). Moreover, when asked what wages they would require to take a job in Yugoslavia, the respondent's average answer was 50 percent greater than the earnings of the average worker in Yugoslavia—although much less than the average Yugoslav worker earns in Germany. In 1970, the average wage in Croatia was 1,254 dinars monthly. The mean response of the Croatian workers as to what would be necessary for them to remain at home was 1,820 dinars, while their average salary in Germany was the equivalent of 3,300 dinars [1971, p. 45].

We have presented thus far an explanation of the Yugoslav migration phenomenon in which the political possibility of migration and an individual's awareness of external migration as an attractive option are essential preconditions for migration. *Given* those conditions, Yugoslav migration decisions have been driven largely by economic considerations, an understanding of which is best achieved by viewing Yugoslavia as part of a larger economic system. Those economic considerations are of two kinds: the availability of jobs primarily in Western Europe, and the gap between income levels in Yugoslavia and elsewhere. With such an approach we can "explain" a picture of the Yugoslav migration circa 1970 characterized by the following two attributes:

1). Yugoslavs from the northern republics, especially persons from Croatia and ethnic Croatians, were most likely to populate the seventh republic.

2). The most insular and least modern republics, Montenegro and Kosovo, have been least represented in the migration flows; the relation between nonmodernity and nonmigration was likewise reflected in the disproportionately small role of women in the already-modest migration of those from the more traditional southern republics.

There is a respect, however, in which this is a rather modest claim from a scholarly viewpoint. It is not surprising that the explanation provides a good fit precisely with that data since it was precisely on the basis, largely, of that data that the explanation was founded. Rather, our explanation should fit other known data about trends in Yugoslav migration patterns and permit an extrapolation of trends through the 1980s. As it turns out, this is the case as regards republic-level data about migration patterns in the period between the 1971 and 1981 censuses, despite the fact of the recession in Europe in the 1970s.

In the 1960s, Slovenia was a major source of migrant workers in Western Europe. Even in 1970 its gross social product per capita (GDP) was $1,848 in 1970 dollars [Vinski, 1972], and its unemployment was among the lowest in Europe. Assuming, with Grecic, that $1,400 in 1970 dollars represented a kind of break-even point for migration, migration should have already peaked at the time of the 1971 census and decreased even further throughout the intervening decade. Table 4.7 reveals that in the very beginning years of the Yugoslav migration, Slovenes were way overrepresented in the outflow, constituting some 16 percent of the total for 1960-1961, and 13 percent for 1965-1966. By 1970-1971, that proportion had decreased to less than 5 percent of the total going abroad annually. The total number of Slovenes abroad continued to diminish steadily throughout the 1970s as few Slovenes went abroad and as Slovenes (along with Croats) returned in disproportionate numbers from abroad. This was scarcely surprising given Slovenia's economy in the 1970s. In 1971 there were slightly less than 15,000 people looking for jobs in Slovenia (Macedonia with a comparable population had more than 57,000). In the ensuing decade, the number looking for work in Slovenia never exceeded 12,500, while (to continue the comparison) in Macedonia that number grew steadily, exceeding 126,000 by 1981 [Statisticki godisjnak Jugoslavije, 1982, p. 450]. Likewise, the median GDP in Slovenia remained twice the Yugoslav average and well above the immigration-emigration equilibrium point throughout the decade—this despite the fact that for Slovenia, as for Yugoslavia as a whole, real personal incomes were only slightly better in 1981 than in 1970 or 1971, having decreased substantially following 1978 [*Statisticki godisnjak Jugoslavije*, 1978, p. 133; 1982, p. 142]. By 1981, there had been an absolute decrease in the number of Slovenians abroad (41,800, from 44,000), and a smaller percentage (2.2 percent) of the Slovenian population was abroad than from any other republic or autonomous region except for the most insular ones, Montenegro and Kosovo, where only 1.7 percent and 1.8 percent of the population were working abroad.

If we treat interrepublic and international migration equally, Slovenia is now a land of immigration—a net importer of labor—rather than one of emigration. Yugoslav observers noted as early as 1971 [Suvar, 1971, p. 1,567] that the "foreign" work force in Slovenia was actually a higher proportion of the total population than in Germany, and such has continued to be the situation. Indeed, a literature concerning the Yugoslav workers in Slovenia has arisen; not surprisingly, it profiles workers from the poorer places in Yugoslavia occupying roles in the Slovenian economy comparable to that of the *gastarbeiter* in Germany.

It was in Croatia, however, that the greatest changes were manifest in the decade separating the 1971 and 1981 censuses. As in Slovenia, the proportion of people from Croatia going abroad in specific years diminished steadily between 1960 and 1971, though they were still a very large fraction of the total migration and, in contrast to workers from Slovenia, constituted a disproportionately large fraction of the annual migration, even in 1971.

Croatia's GDP—$865 in 1965—was well below the $1,400 GNP equilibrium figure. By 1970 it was $1,235. Its GDP then hovered close to $1,400 throughout the 1971-1981 period, even exceeding it in the most prosperous years of the time span, 1978-1979. Unlike Slovenia, however, Croatia's unemployment increased significantly from 42,000 to 86,000 over the period, though these were figures that were modest compared with those in less developed Yugoslav republics [*Statisticki godisnjak Jugoslavije*, 1982]. The decade 1971-1981 witnessed a dramatic decrease in the number of Croatians working abroad. The Yugoslav census data reveal that there were some 73,000 fewer Croatian workers abroad in 1981 than in 1971, despite the fact that the 1981 census counts only 46,000 fewer Yugoslav workers abroad. As a result, the outmigration of Croatians has basically stabilized and the external migration is no longer a primarily Croatian phenomenon, even if the demand for workers in Western Europe should revive. Rather, Croatia in the 1980s is increasingly likely to be as preoccupied with the problems that attend the outmigration of workers from other regions of Yugoslavia as with the problems that accompany the outmigration of workers abroad from Croatia.

On the basis of the data resulting from the 1971 census, Vojvodina seems to occupy a place intermediate between Slovenia and Croatia and the less developed regions of Yugoslavia. Between 1971 and 1981, the number of persons from Vojvodina abroad decreased significantly. Using Yugoslav sources, there were 20 percent fewer persons from Vojvodina working abroad in 1981 than there were in 1971, and its GDP per capita was only a few hundred dollars (in constant 1970 dollars) below the hypothetical migration equilibrium point. Unemployment is high, however, and it would seem that there could be some modest, temporary reinvigoration of migration abroad in response to strong demand from Western Europe, although it seems unlikely ever to reachieve the 1971 level. Indeed, over the course of the 1980s, given the revival of the Yugoslav economy, migration from Vojvodina may gradually decline.

The most striking characteristic of the seventh republic as portrayed by the 1981 census when compared with the 1971 census is the extent to which it became a Serbian rather than a Croatian phenomenon. The reduced demand for *gastarbeiter* notwithstanding, there were about 50,000 more persons from Serbia proper abroad in the 1981 enumeration than there were in 1971. By a small amount, the number of persons abroad from Serbia proper (152,932 people, 24.5 percent of the total) exceeded that from Croatia (151,619 people, 24.3 percent of the total) in 1981. With more than 260,000 in Serbia proper looking for work (by contrast, Croatia with four-fifths the population had 86,000 unemployed in 1981) and a GDP of roughly $1,000 per capita in 1970 dollars, it is easy to imagine a considerable growth of migration abroad from the poorer areas of Serbia proper in response to a reviving West European economy. Ultimately, by the early 1990s, a gradual decline will become noticeable as the more prosperous areas of Serbia proper absorb the bulk of the migration flows.

In the two less developed republics, Bosnia-Hercegovina and Macedonia, where knowledge of migration abroad as an alternative is of long standing, migration remains a highly attractive option, assuming the recovery of the West European economy. In Bosnia-Hercegovina, where migration had already assumed major proportions prior to 1971, there was a slight decrease in the number of workers abroad during the 1971-1981 decade (134,000 rather than 137,000). How much that was a product of events in the global economy rather than events in Bosnia-Hercegovina may be judged by the fact that the number of persons seeking employment in Bosnia-Hercegovina grew from 32,500 to 143,000 during the same time span [*Statisticki godisnjak Jugoslavije*, 1982, p. 450]. With a GDP per capita in 1981 (in 1970 dollars) of less than $700, a revival in the West European economy would almost certainly result in renewed major migratory outflows.

The situation for Macedonia is much the same as in Bosnia-Hercegovina.

During the decade 1971-1981, we witness basically the same stability in the number abroad as in Bosnia-Hercegovina; there is a slight increase in the Macedonian population abroad and a correspondingly slight decrease in the representation in the citizenry from Bosnia-Hercegovina abroad. In Macedonia, unemployment is staggeringly high and becoming worse. We have already noted that there were more than ten times as many people seeking work at the end of 1981 in Macedonia than there were in the comparably sized but vastly more industrialized Slovenia. Almost equally suggestive is the fact that in Bosnia-Hercegovina, which has roughly the same GDP per capita as Macedonia and more than twice the population, there were only 16,500 more unemployed (143,000 rather than 126,500). The likelihood that Macedonia under conditions of a European economic recovery will be a source for greater outmigration of workers in the 1980s and 1990s seems consequently quite strong.

In percentage terms, however, where the big migration boom is likely to occur in the 1980s and 1990s is in Montenegro and Kosovo. During the 1971-1981 period, the number of workers from each republic increased significantly in percentage terms. Despite the recession in Europe, the number of people from Montenegro abroad increased by one-quarter (24.9 percent) between 1971 and 1981, and the number from Kosovo increased by a little less than one-fifth (18.9 percent) in the same period. Both Montenegro and Kosovo, however, remain quite underrepresented in the seventh republic in comparison with their respective populations [Baucic, 1982, p. 331].

Against the backdrop of a European recovery, there are several reasons why we should expect the big changes in external migration trends to occur in Montenegro and especially in Kosovo. Communication linkages are developing rapidly in Yugoslavia. The gap between, for instance, radio listenership and newspaper readership that separates the less developed republics and Kosovo from Croatia and Slovenia is less than the gap that separates the median income per capita in the northern and southern republics. Over time, moreover, the migration has become increasingly institutionalized, and knowledge of opportunities for employment has become increasingly diffused through formal rather than informal personal networks. Likewise, the process of de-agrarianization will continue in the 1980s in Kosovo and Montenegro, whereas many of the departures from the village had already occurred in the northern republics. Interethnic tensions between Serbs and Albanians may also contribute to the outmigration, but the analysis here presumes that the propensity for migration exists independent of such tensions. Finally, the Yugoslav government is far less likely to curb the migration of unskilled workers or land-poor villagers than they are the skilled workers from Belgrade or Zagreb.

In general, consequently, the profile of those abroad in 1981 far more closely resembles the Yugoslav mean than did the 1971 profile. The 1981 census reveals a profile in which the most developed republic, Slovenia, and the least modernized republics, Kosovo and Montenegro, are underrepresented. This is a picture entirely consonant with the explanation adopted herein: relatively modest modernization of Kosovo and Montenegro meshes with low migration as does Slovenia's prosperity. The great overrepresentation of persons from Croatia and, we must assume pending the availability of more refined results from the 1981 census, of ethnic Croatians has dissipated substantially. Representation of Croatians abroad in 1981 is no longer, as it was in 1971, way out of line with what one would expect on a random basis. The trend in this regard for the 1980s is surely toward, not away from, the mean. Instead, as Serbians from Montenegro and Kosovo, as well as from Serbia proper and Vojvodina, continue to go abroad in the 1980s, it is more likely that the migration phenomenon will be a source of discomfort for Serbian nationalists rather than, as was the case in 1971, for Croatian nationalists. We have seen that the population of the seventh republic, especially when both workers and nonworking members of workers families are included, has not changed substantially between 1971 and 1981, despite the most severe economic recession in Europe since World War II. Partly this is because those abroad with jobs have stayed far longer than the notion ''temporary'' could ever subsume. In addition, far more nonworking Yugoslavs have gone abroad to join their working spouse or father. Others went abroad during the 1970s despite the bad economic situation in Europe.

As a consequence, the outmigration of Yugoslav workers remains a central issue for Yugoslavia as a whole in much the way it did at the outset of the 1970s, though the problems have become somewhat different as the nature of the migration has changed. It is far less a concern for the northern republics than it was in 1971—at least as far as the prospect of an increase in the number of migrant workers is concerned. (Problems of reintegrating workers and their children in, for instance, Croatian society after stays of a decade or more are another matter.) Yugoslav decisionmakers found themselves, in the period after 1971, confronted with the tasks of dealing with the policy and political implications of the existence of the seventh republic as a basically fixed feature of the Yugoslav polity. With the prospect that a new wave of migration from the Yugoslav south is probable as Western Europe recovers economically, they will continue to find themselves in the same position, at least until the next census in 1991.

That seventh republic is, of course, outside the formal territorial confines of Yugoslavia, a manifestation of the linkages between the Yugoslav and the more general international labor market. Its size has remained strikingly constant since 1971, despite the global stagflation of the 1970s. As such, it has enormous political implications for Yugoslav elite-mass relations and poses for Yugoslav elites an exceedingly difficult question, namely, how in such circumstances do they govern the seventh republic. It is to the political implications of openness and the task of governing the seventh republic that we now turn.

5

GOVERNING THE SEVENTH REPUBLIC
AND THE POLITICAL CONSEQUENCES
OF OPENNESS

Both economic and political considerations motivated the opening of the Yugoslav borders in the first half of the 1960s and the consequent outmigration of Yugoslav workers—an outmigration amounting, by the early 1970s, to roughly a million workers, or one-fifth of the work force. The total number of Yugoslavs abroad remained basically constant throughout the decade following the stagflation and recession precipitated by the 1973 jump in global oil prices. The result was the emergence, as a basically stable part of the Yugoslav political scene, of a seventh republic with twice the population of Montenegro. Yugoslavs resided in this seventh republic for varying periods of time. A few—5 per cent in a 1977 survey (see Table 5.1)—stayed less than a year, and only one-quarter stayed for up to three years. More typically, the stay was from four to seven years. Some stayed even longer. The 1977 survey revealed that close to one-tenth (9.7 per cent) had been abroad for eight to nine years prior to returning to Yugoslavia, and that nearly as many (8.7 per cent) had resided in the seventh republic for ten or more years prior to returning. As we have noted, for most Yugoslavs, "temporary" was a very long time.

The duration of the typical stay abroad meant that the seventh republic was a place where Yugoslav citizens lived for a sizable fraction of their lives; where children were born, raised—some speaking only German or Swedish—and went to school. It was a place where a sizable fraction of the Yugoslavs resided, who in a crisis could be called upon to fight—Tito in 1972 spoke of "three big armies" [Borba, December 9, 1972]. It was also a place where the major media were independent of Yugoslav authorities, where the mores of modern Western industrial capitalism and "bourgeois" democracy prevailed, and where there existed and operated groups fundamentally opposed to the Yugoslav idea, to communism, or to both.

This chapter addresses two questions about the seventh republic. 1) How is that seventh republic "governed"? 2) What are the consequences of the existence of the seventh republic and its linkages to Yugoslav political institutions and society for the Yugoslav political system, and especially for mass-elite relations within the territorial confines of Yugoslavia?

106

TABLE 5.1
Returnees by Years Abroad (In percentages)

Time Abroad in Years	Returning Percentages	Time Abroad in Years	Returning Percentages	Time Abroad in Years	Returning Percentages
1	5.0	5	16.0	9	3.5
2	7.6	6	15.6	10	3.8
3	12.5	7	11.5	More than 10	4.9
4	13.4	8	6.2		100.0

SOURCE: Nejasmic [1981], p. 30. The N for the survey was 822 returning migrants from Bosnia-Hercegovina, Croatia, and Serbia. No data were provided for the number of nonrespondents to this question.

GOVERNING THE SEVENTH REPUBLIC

When political scientists and plain people speak of governing, they usually have a number of things in mind. The political science literature is replete with attempts to articulate in fairly all-embracing forms various conceptions of the political system and its functioning [see Almond in Jacobson and Zimmerman, eds., 1969; Rosenau, 1971].

Governing has a minimal notion of steering and the legitimate use of coercion. States govern when they extract resources from their citizens, or take plunder from others. States govern when they regulate or control the behavior of their own citizens through the use of police and when they provide security against external or internal threats posed by other armed corporate actors whether they be national liberation movements or other states. They govern, too, when they attempt to shape the directions of investment, the consumer's marginal propensity to spend, or the distribution of wealth. These things modern states usually do through a complex set of incentives, subsidies, and sanctions. They govern when they provide services unrelated to protection—whether these services be education, medical care, or social welfare. Finally, states govern when they pursue measures that develop and/or maintain citizen attachments to key values and institutions. These attachments may be to the state itself—the fatherland or motherland. They may be to key political institutions that are an integral part of the definition of the state—Americans pledge allegiance to the flag of the United States of America and to the republic for which it stands. Likewise, the attachment may be to particular values—to socialism or to the free enterprise system, or to a particular religious variant. States may accomplish such political socialization, moreover, by civic training in the schools, by controlling the media flows or sources, and by systematic generation of information and

107

propaganda. Some states accomplish these purposes by encouraging participation in, or the illusion of participation in, the process of governing itself.

With slight qualification, it may be said that the Yugoslav authorities gave little initial thought to governing the outmigration of workers. Rather, the initial decisions are better viewed as intended to remove the issue of exit from the province of the authorities concern. In 1963-1964 travel restrictions were gradually reduced, with the major restriction being that an individual seeking to go abroad had to have completed his military service and had to contribute to the maintenance of his family at home. The passport reform implemented in 1966 and 1967 provided the political and institutional context that opened the borders. With the adoption of the economic reforms, migration was no longer condemned as it had been before 1962, nor tolerated as it was in the years from 1962 to 1965. Rather, it was positively encouraged.

Between 1966 and 1972, the Yugoslav authorities dealt with the workers abroad in two main ways. Prior to 1966, no assistance was provided the worker who was searching for a job abroad. With the Amendment of the Law on the Organization and Financing of Employment [*Sluzbeni list*, No. 47, 1966], federal, republic, and local employment bureaus were charged with the responsibility of organizing the overflow of Yugoslav workers and of matching the supply of Yugoslav workers with the needs of foreign firms. This was a large endeavor: "From the regional services to the federal bureaus, special departments or working groups were formed which were, in many cases, more numerous and more involved in their task than some parts of the employment services mediating employment in Yugoslavia" [Ines Kozina in OECD, *Joint Project*, 1975, p. 52]. Moreover, as Ms. Kozina notes, the activities of the employment bureaus were not limited merely to contacting foreign employers or employment agencies. Rather, they "followed the labour market closely . . . worked out bilateral agreements and conventions with the receiving countries; [and] elaborated the collective contracts" [OECD, *Joint Project*, 1975, p. 52]. They also organized vocational training programs. In short, the Yugoslav Employment Bureaus aided the Yugoslav citizens in finding jobs abroad and sought to negotiate arrangements that would assure that the foreign authorities and firms would provide minimum standards for them while abroad. In general, however, the relationship was one in which arrangements were made and the Yugoslavs departed to work in a foreign country. By accepting foreign employment, "the link between the employment service and the migrant [was] broken." This is not to say there were no contacts between the employment services and the migrant once the migrant was abroad. "Representatives of the employment services visited our migrants, in some cases very frequently"; but these contacts were motivated primarily "by the goal of securing further employment for new workers" [OECD, *Joint Project*, 1975, p. 53].

The other major method by which the Yugoslav authorities provided assistance to the workers abroad in the years from 1966 to 1972 was through conventional foreign policy means. This took two forms: from 1964 on, the Yugoslav consulates were available to provide advice as to how migrants could "obtain assistance in solving various problems concerning their life and work in the host countries, and new consulates were opened in response to the workers' needs, including thirteen in West Germany alone between 1964 and 1973" [Baucic, 1975, p. 18]. The other means, again one typically associated with foreign policy, was the negotiation of bilateral treaties. Yugoslavia negotiated eight bilateral treaties on the regulation of the employment of Yugoslav workers in France (1965), Austria and Sweden (1966), West Germany (1969), and Belgium, The Netherlands, Luxembourg, and Australia (1970). By 1969, the Federal Secretariat for Labor and Social Policy, along with the Ministry of Foreign Affairs, the Federal Bureau for Employment, and the Yugoslav Committee for Disabled and Old Age Pension Insurance, had succeeded in negotiating provisions for health, old-age pensions, and disability insurance with almost all the West European states receiving migrants.

The picture that emerges of Yugoslav handling of migrant workers between 1965 and 1972 is one informed by an implicit, rather conventional, view of the realms of domestic and foreign affairs, and of the role of the state domestically and abroad. Workers had the opportunity to be advised before they departed. Their conditions abroad were monitored largely in order to pave the way for future departures. While they were abroad, the major means of attending to the workers' concerns was through bilateral state-to-state or multilateral treaties or through the consulates—that is, through the conventional means the state has of dealing with the protection of its citizens outside the territorial confines of the state, in this instance, Yugoslavia.

In only two respects was this pattern divergent from conventional conceptions of relations among modern social welfare states. In addition to the bilateral treaties, there also existed early on a set of well-developed relations between Yugoslav and West European trade unions.

The Yugoslav Alliance of Labour Unions (SSJ) has, from the beginning of the organized employment of Yugoslav workers in foreign countries, shown great initiative and helped the development of cooperation with trade unions of host countries. It made great efforts to engage the foreign trade unions, especially in the practical realizations of the rights of the Yugoslav workers at their place of employment. . . .

109

There is a permanent joint committee of the SSJ . . . with the associations of the trade unions of Germany (DGB), Sweden (LO), and Austria (OeGB), which meets at least once a year. . . . Especially close cooperation exists between the SSJ and the DGB. At the DGB there is a Bureau for Yugoslav Workers with two permanent representatives from the SSJ. The SSJ is encouraging Yugoslav workers to become members of the trade unions in host coutries. In Austria and Sweden, about 90% of the Yugoslav workers are members of trade unions, and in the Federal Republic of Germany, about 20% [Baucic, 1975, pp. 20-21].

In addition, modest efforts were made from 1964 on to provide special radio programs, to organize cultural and entertainment programs for the workers abroad, to insert supplements in some weeklies, the most influential of which was *VUS* (*Vjesnik u srijedu*). (*VUS* was closed down, as excessively nationalistic, after the 1971 Zagreb student strike.) In general, though, the picture for the years 1965 to 1972 is one of Yugoslav authorities governing the workers *prior* to their departure and negotiating with the Western European states and Australia about the ways *those states* would govern the workers during their stay abroad.

Developments relating directly to the workers' migration, and ones bearing only tangentially on that migration, combined in 1973-1974 to produce a series of measures and declarations relating to multiple aspects of the migration flow. Among the most important were the resolution adopted at the joint session of the LCY Presidency and the Presidency of the Yugoslav government (February 5, 1973), the resolution on employment adopted at the Tenth LCY Congress in 1974, the Law on Basic Conditions for the Temporary Employment and the Protection of Yugoslav Citizens Employed Abroad [*Sluzbeni list*, No. 33, 1973], and the Social Compact on the Temporary Employment of Yugoslav Citizens Employed Abroad [*Sluzbeni list*, No. 39, 1974].

From one perspective, these laws were restrictive. The regulations adopted in the late 1960s had focused on the process by which employment abroad was achieved, and the treaties negotiated had regulated the conditions under which Yugoslavs abroad actually worked. Similarly, the rules in the late 1960s paid little attention to the social consequences of migration, but rather facilitated individual choices. Whereas in the late 1960s virtually any Yugoslav could choose to go abroad to work under the auspices of the Federal Bureau for Employment without regard to the consequences, the legislation adopted in the early 1970s was addressed "not only to the interests of the migrants, but to societal [*drustveni*] interests, as well" [Baucic, 1979, p. 10]. (There was still nothing to prevent someone from going shopping in Trieste and not returning.) Thus, military service had to be completed prior to the departure, and in 1974 reserve officers were not permitted to leave. Financial support and schooling of children left behind also had to be assured. Moreover, persons refusing employment in Yugoslavia would be denied a permit to go abroad. There was a clear developmental thrust to the legislation: the intent was to export the unskilled and the unemployed, rather than the employed and skilled. (This had also been the economic rationale for opening the borders in the mid-1960s in the aftermath of the 1965 reforms, but as we saw, both unskilled and skilled, unemployed and employed, departed.) The 1974 Social Agreement makes explicit reference to those in "endangered occupations" who may be denied permits. Finally, the laws for the first time made mention of the need to ensure the return and reintegration of the workers into Yugoslav society.

These new rules reflected an awareness that the original vision of the migration as "a *temporary* need of one part of the population of working age to take up *temporary* employment" [Baucic, 1978, p. 5; italics in original] abroad was misconceived. The migration was hardly confined to one part of the population of working age—it was a mass phenomenon. Equally to the point, the migration was neither temporary in the sense that the migration of Yugoslavs, as a phenomenon, was going to be of relatively brief duration, nor in the sense that when individual Yugoslavs went abroad their stay was relatively brief.

Most of what Yugoslav analysts and policymakers increasingly identified, correctly or not, as negative consequences of migration were a result of the nontemporary nature of the outflow. Baucic [1978, p. 7] has a nice list of the negative effects of migration that were becoming apparent in the early 1970s: the departure of skilled workers (often of those skills in which Yugoslavia itself was undersupplied) resulted in "the postponement of return, different forms of alienation amongst a section of migrants, irrational utilization of the migrants' savings and remittances, social problems of the families of migrants, unfavourable effects on the defence capacity of the country, and so on." Most of these related quite directly not only to the magnitude of the outflow, but to the duration of the stay abroad.

The changes in the practices regarding migration also were conditioned by broader events. The Soviet invasion of Czechoslovakia in 1968 and U.S.-Soviet détente in the early 1970s reinforced Yugoslav beliefs that Yugoslavia would have to look primarily to its own resources in the event of an external threat. Within Yugoslavia, the reconsideration of the migration policy was framed against the backdrop of the Croatian mass movement in 1971 and the student strike in Zagreb—a strike that had been timed initially to coincide with the Christmas–New Year vacations of the *gastarbeiter*— and subsequent events. Of these, certain domestic events occurring in 1972

111

were specially relevant: they included the publication of Tito's famous "Letter" with its emphasis on Leninist themes and the ouster of liberal republic party officials amidst public attacks on those with excessively close ties to "Western Europe or Bavaria" [Kardelj, *Borba*, September 22, 1972], most notably Stane Kavcic of Slovenia and Marko Nikezic of Serbia. Internationally, the 1973 Arab-induced oil shock and the subsequent recession and stagflation in Europe were, by bringing home reminders of the costs of global interdependence, especially noteworthy.

A common thread runs through all the legislation adopted in the early 1970s. By virtue of the migrants' being abroad in large numbers for a long duration, and as a relatively permanent feature of the Yugoslav scene, it would be necessary to act in ways to link the migrants to Yugoslavia, and to assure that approximately the same duties were exacted from, and roughly analogous benefits afforded to, those Yugoslav citizens working abroad as those living within Yugoslavia. This implied that for many purposes Yugoslav decisionmakers had to act as though there really were a seventh republic, and to deal with its residents not merely before they left the country, or through foreign policy instruments such as consulates, treaties, and international conventions. Instead, the Yugoslav decisionmakers acted increasingly as though they had to treat the workers, while abroad, as nearly as possible as a matter of domestic politics. The Yugoslav government began to implement measures to govern the migrants—to control, to inform, to socialize, etc.—while they were abroad, rather than limiting itself to measures prior to departure, or to negotiations with West Germany or Sweden about how the migrant workers would be governed by those states. In the mid-1960s, Karl Deutsch [Farrell, ed., 1966, pp. 8, 9, 12] spoke of a linkage group as a "subsystem of the national community" "more weakly bonded against [the international environment] and more receptive to outside inputs" and which has "particular links to the international or foreign input." At the time I regarded that as a rather restrictive definition; my sense was that it was preferable to think of a linkage group as any group of citizens—corporate or otherwise—of the state in question with direct linkages to the international environment, i.e., linkages unmediated by the state. In this broader definition it would be an entirely empirical question whether a linkage group was located wholly or partially within, or external to, the confines of the domestic system. By the broader definition, one could treat as linkage groups American multinational corporations that do 80 percent of their business abroad, the Spanish communist party when its leadership was in exile, and the Turkish and Yugoslav workers in West Germany. Deutsch's conception seemed to impede clear thinking. Surely, it seemed to me on first reading, if the Turkish workers are in Germany, it was better to think of them as outside the boundaries of the Turkish system than to depict

112

Turkey, a half-century after the collapse of the Ottoman Empire, and almost three hundred years after the Turks fell back from the siege of Vienna, as extending to Vienna, Munich, and Frankfurt.

At the time the Deutsch paper appeared (1966), it was appropriate to characterize the Yugoslav workers as a linkage group in the broader sense suggested here, but not in Deutsch's more narrow construction. Abroad, they had direct linkages to the external environment, almost entirely unmediated by the state; but by virtue of their being abroad, it made little sense to treat them as a "subsystem of the national community" "more weakly bonded against the international environment." Dating from roughly 1972, it became increasingly appropriate to regard the Yugoslav workers as a linkage group in Deutsch's more narrow sense. In Baucic's words, "the sociopolitical organizations and administrative bodies in Yugoslavia came to the conclusion that the foreign migrants are a *specific category of the population*" [Baucic, 1976, p. 19; italics added]. What the migrants lacked was the whole network of institutions of a modern, in this case, authoritarian, welfare state. Baucic describes the lacunae with reference to social welfare and social work, but the point is a more general one: "In the country, social activities are not only carried out in specialized social welfare institutions such as welfare centers, but also in the work of virtually all organized social units ranging from work organizations, sports and cultural clubs, residential organizations (*mjesne zajednice*) to various agencies—employment, health and social welfare—and to republic or provincial and federal social, political, and administrational agencies" [Baucic, 1976, p. 19].

Governing the workers abroad involved the search for ways to provide surrogates for such institutions and to accomplish the functions such institutions conventionally play to a "specific category of the population" of Yugoslavia that happened not to be located in any of the six republics. This is not to assert that all the tasks subsumed under the rubric of "governing" the seventh republic were accomplished by means that implied the near absence of boundaries between the six republics and the seventh. In many instances the modalities employed remained as they had been: rules were set that applied at departure or on return, and negotiations continued to be undertaken that entailed traditional foreign policy modalities and resulted in rules, conventions, or practices adopted by other states. Nevertheless, the breadth of matters treated and the means often employed in the 1970s bespoke a conception of the workers abroad and the manner of dealing with them that implied a kind of novel transnationalism. What we witnessed was an overlapping of the effective, as opposed to *de jure*, boundaries of Yugoslavia with those of other states, especially Europe. This was really quite remarkable—at least for those accustomed to envisaging the world of states as a place characterized by mutually exclusive jurisdictions, or to those who, while realizing that the billiard-ball model [Wolfers, 1962] no longer operates (if it ever did), associate political penetration with the behavior and influence of great states on small powers [Rosenau in Farrell, ed., 1966].

With regard to the extractive dimensions of governing, the Yugoslavs did little that revealed any fundamentally novel conception of the links between Yugoslavia and the international system. Early on, the Yugoslav authorities realized that the migrant workers had become Yugoslavia's chief export. Remittances from abroad were and remain a very sizable fraction of all hard currency earnings (see Tables 5.2 and 5.3), even though the decrease in the value of European currencies against the dollar doubtless reduced the value of remittances in the mid-1980s.

When it comes to customs regulations, however, Yugoslav authorities have made it clear that the workers abroad are not to be treated as are other Yugoslavs. There are obvious economic reasons why this is so. The point here is that they have, legally, a special status that differentiates them from other Yugoslavs abroad. Moreover, the point extends to efforts to regulate the outflow of Yugoslavs undertaken in the fall of 1982. At that juncture, as a tentative measure, the Yugoslav Federal Executive Committee ruled that a 5,000-dinar "deposit" would be required of all Yugoslavs leaving the country, an amount that increased by 2,000-dinar increments with each subsequent trip. There were exceptions to that rule, however, for business travel, some local border traffic, and, for our purposes most relevantly, for the workers going back abroad to their pre-existing jobs in Western Europe. With respect to customs privileges per se, moreover, "all . . . privileges . . . [are] abolished with the exception of those for workers temporarily working abroad who are definitely returning home" [*FBIS*, October 19, 1982, p. I 7].

In the case of military service, a chief obligation of citizenship, the manner of controlling the workers abroad has been fairly conventional. From the 1970s the rules have precluded departures prior to the completion of mili-

TABLE 5.2
Remittances in Millions of U.S. Dollars

Year	Source A	Source B	Year	Source A	Source B
1971	716.1	772.9	1976	1,878.2	1,883.7
1972	963.8	1,051.3	1977	2,097.0	2,097.2
1973	1,397.7	1,397.7	1978	2,898.9	2,890.0
1974	1,621.4	1,621.4	1979	3,216.3	3,393.0
1975	1,695.8	1,695.8	1980	4,791.0	43,050.0

SOURCES: A. OECD [1982], p. 199. B. Cicin-Sain [1983], pp. 165-173.

TABLE 5.3

The Share of Remittances from Workers Abroad in the Yugoslav International
Balance of Payments (In millions of U. S. dollars)

	1963	1974	1977	1980
Expenditures				
Imports of goods	1,021	7,531	9,700	14,309
Other expenditures	131	1,073	1,968	5,163
Total	1,152	8,604	11,668	19,472
Income				
Exports	737	4,104	5,445	9,269
Tourism	53	699	841	1,115
Remittances*	41	1,621	2,097	4,791
Other	110	941	1,183	1,777
Total	941	7,365	9,566	17,952
% remittances of the total				
of all earnings	4.4%	22.0%	21.9%	26.7%

SOURCES: Baucic [1979], p. 21; OECD [1982], p. 200.
*From workers abroad and emigrants.

tary service and have forbidden the departure of reserve officers. The service is extracted prior to, and is a condition of, departure.

The police function of the state is, on the other hand, exercised as regards Yugoslavs, including workers, abroad primarily on their return. Persons are sentenced for engaging in such crimes by Yugoslav lights as "hostile propaganda" while outside Yugoslavia—in the United States, in Canada, and in Western Europe. Thus one Vjekoslav Mihalic is reported to have been sentenced in 1982 to a year in Zagreb for "hostile activities against SFRY while in Sweden" [CADDY, *Bulletin*, No. 1, 1983, p. 1], and one Milutin Vutin was arrested in Banja Luka in 1983 on his return from Austria for "associating with political emigres" [CADDY, *Bulletin*, No. 19, 1983, p. 2].

It is very likely that the Yugoslav secret police operate outside the *de jure* boundaries of Yugoslavia and engage in a kind of governance of the seventh republic in this manner. The CADDY *Bulletin*, which, while explicitly hostile to Yugoslav communism, appears to provide reasonably extensive coverage of such matters, reports an interesting and relevant episode: "Josip Majerski, 37, went to the Federal Republic of Germany in 1970 as a guest worker from Yugoslavia. In 1976 he was granted political asylum, and in early July 1983, he either was arrested or defected, as an agent of the Yugoslav secret service. . . . Upon reaching Germany, Majerski joined a number of emigre groups and became a most vocal nationalist, instigating fellow emigres to undertake terrorist acts against the regime representatives abroad. Preliminary interrogation of Majerski indicates he was connected with at least ten murders of exiles in Europe, kidnappings from Europe to Yugoslavia, and arrests of returnees when they arrived home'' [CADDY, *Bulletin*, No. 19, 1983, pp. 2-3].

More conventional evidence that the Yugoslav authorities have been concerned with the governance of the seventh republic is to be found in the area of political socialization and resocialization of Yugoslavs abroad. Here the Yugoslavs have actively sought to retain or ensure the loyalties of their citizens resident in the seventh republic. This has the potential of becoming a considerable problem. Some of the available evidence lends credence to the common-sense notion that duration abroad has a direct bearing on attitude change. Resocialization appears to accelerate progressively with number of years abroad. (Unfortunately, the only data touching on this subject are not time series data but rather the responses of different people who have been abroad for different durations.) Zvonimir Komarica [1970], in his discussion of the findings of an unpublished survey of Yugoslav workers, finds consolation in the fact that only 12.2 per cent of the Yugoslav workers who were abroad responded that each would rather be a ''small proprietor abroad than a well-paid worker in Yugoslavia.'' By contrast, 84.8 per cent indicated that they would prefer to be well-paid workers in Yugoslavia rather than small proprietors abroad (3 per cent did not answer). For our purposes, however, what is interesting is that of those who answered, 5 per cent who had been abroad for less than six months chose ''small proprietor abroad,'' 16 per cent of those abroad between a year and three years answered ''small proprietor abroad,'' and 27 per cent of those abroad more than three years expressed their preference for being a small proprietor abroad rather than a well-paid worker at home. Other questions in the survey point to the same conclusion: workers abroad for more than three years are more prone to advise children to go abroad to work, more likely to read the emigrant press, and less disposed to join a workers' organization abroad composed of Yugoslav workers (see Table 5.4) [Komarica, 1970, pp. 5-6, 45]. In addition, another source indicates that persons abroad are less well informed about political activities in Yugoslavia. Table 5.5 reports the survey results for Croatians in Croatia and abroad, and indicates the frequencies of those who were well informed, averagely informed, and poorly informed about social-political activities in Yugoslavia.

However, the evidence does not all point in the same direction. Those who spend an extended time abroad are not necessarily acquiring attitudes that are antithetical to the prevailing Yugoslav political culture. An indication of the strength of the pulls of home and the homeland—though not necessarily of typically Yugoslav political themes—is that Croatian workers abroad in 1970 indicated that on the average they would rather work in Yugoslavia for 1,820 dinars a month at a time when their average salary in Ger-

TABLE 5.4
Time Abroad and Attitudinal Preferences (In percentages)

Time Abroad	Abroad	Yugoslavia	Would You Advise Your Children to Go Abroad to Work?	
			Yes	No
6 months or less	5	95	15	81
6 months to 1 year	7	93	13	82
1 year to 3 years	16	84	21	77
3 years or more	27	73	33	60

Time Abroad	Do You Read Emigrant Press?		Do You Participate in Yugoslav Workers' Organizations?	
	Yes	No	Yes	No
6 months or less	25	75	87	13
6 months to 1 year	27	73	88	12
1 year to 3 years	49	51	86	14
3 years or more	48	52	78	22

TABLE 5.5
Level of Socio-Political Information among Persons in Croatia,
and Croatians Abroad (In percentages)

Level of Informedness	Residing in Croatia	Croatians Working Abroad
High	21.4%	9.9%
Medium	50.8	48.0
Low	27.8	41.8
Unknown	—	0.3
N =	588	1,340
(Chi square = 63.1, p is less than .01)		

SOURCE: Letic, [1977], p. 66.

many was the equivalent of 3,300 dinars [Baucic and Maravic, 1971, p. 45].

More direct evidence that the experience abroad may at least, for some Yugoslavs, intensify their attachment to key Yugoslav norms is provided by survey data from Slovenian studies conducted in Yugoslavia and in Germany. Slovenes were asked a series of questions relating to their evaluation of migration. Among the most relevant for addressing the issue of attitude change were the following: Do you agree or disagree with the statements that

117

a) When "we employ the work force abroad we weaken the defensive power of our country";
b) "People employed abroad send home foreign exchange and thus help Yugoslavia";
c) "Citizens of Yugoslavia that live (temporarily) abroad will abandon socialism for foreign ideas";
d) "Persons who work abroad aid the maintenance of the capitalist system in Europe";
e) "Persons who work abroad will have on the occasion of their return, broader views than those which they left at home";
f) "Employment abroad is a solution for unemployment in the country."

Interestingly, the pattern of responses conveys the strong impression that experience abroad does not decrease attachment to Yugoslav symbols, but if anything somewhat increases identification with Yugoslavia or Slovenia. Table 5.6 displays responses given by the returnees and by nonmigrant Slovenes to the above questions.

The message that emerges is that Slovenes returning from abroad have a somewhat jaded view of the experience, though they recognize the possibility of attitude change while abroad. The returnees are somewhat more disposed to believe both that work abroad aids the maintenance of the capitalist system and that it results in the acceptance of alien ideas. At the same time, they are less inclined to think that work abroad is broadening or a solution to the country's unemployment problems, or that the worker abroad aids the country by sending home hard currency. Perhaps most important, they are slightly more disposed to accept the proposition that exporting the work force weakens the defense capability of the country. For Slovenes, at least, work experience abroad may weaken attachment to socialism, but it does not enamor them with the West.

Recognizing that attitude change abroad may nevertheless be a problem, Yugoslav authorities, beginning in 1970, turned their attention to providing services intended to retain the Yugoslav workers' identity with the homeland and with the "right" values as well as to provide for the political socialization—what in the old days used to be termed "civic training"—of Yugoslav youths abroad.

With respect to the workers themselves, there have emerged a striking number of resources targeted to their edification. The Social Agreement pertaining to the education of Yugoslav workers abroad, first proposed in 1975, was designed to ensure that the curriculum for Yugoslav workers abroad was identical to that in Yugoslavia and that the cadres included in such educational activities would have "certain professional and moral-political qualities." Financing of such ventures, moreover, was to come from the employers and government agencies abroad, the contributions of mi-

TABLE 5.6
Key Attitudes of Slovenes toward Migration: A Comparison

Question	Response	Nonmigrant Slovenes	Returnees
a) Employing the work force	Agree	68%	75%
abroad weakens the country's	Disagree	17	8
defensive power.	Don't know*	15	17
b) The remittances of those	Agree	82%	74%
employed abroad help	Disagree	8	10
Yugoslavia.	Don't know*	9	16
c) People employed abroad	Agree	34%	52%
will abandon socialism	Disagree	42	21
for foreign ideas.	Don't know*	23	27
d) People employed abroad	Agree	42%	55%
are helping maintain the	Disagree	32	20
capitalist system in Europe.	Don't know*	25	25
e) The experience of working	Agree	44%	36%
abroad will broaden the	Disagree	43	45
views of those involved.	Don't know*	13	19
f) Employment abroad is a	Agree	68%	57%
solution for unemployment	Disagree	20	28
at home.	Don't know*	13	15

SOURCE: Silva Meznaric in Tos, et al. [1978], pp. 84-85.
NOTE: Some totals do not equal 100% because of rounding. Chi square = 34.3, 15.6, 94.1, 39.0, 14.2, and 18.5 for questions a, b, c, d, e, and f respectively, all of which are significant at the .001 level. (The chi square test was employed by converting the percentages reported back to what, given the reported sample sizes, were presumably the original Ns.)
*Or no answer.

grant workers, and from a host of Yugoslav local and republic institutions [Mladen Vedris in OECD, *Joint Project*, 1975, pp. 64-65].

Moreover, the media targeted to the Yugoslav workers abroad have become a substantial industry. Radio is especially important in reaching the workers abroad. Studies of Croatians in Croatia and Croatians abroad reveal that those abroad rely primarily on the radio for information, whereas their counterparts at home rely much more heavily on the press (see Table 5.7).

With this in mind, virtually every republic's radio station has a special program in the evening for Yugoslavs abroad: Radio Zagreb produces "Our Citizens in the World" every Saturday. Radio Belgrade has a daily morning information program, "Good Morning, Countrymen" and twice a week—on Tuesdays and Fridays—produces "An Evening Together." Radio Ljubljana produces "Words and Sounds from the Forests of Home"; and Radio Sarajevo "Fridays with You" [Letic, 1973, p. 17].

119

TABLE 5.7

Major Information Source by Media for Persons from Croatia

Media	Croatians Abroad	Croatians at Home
Radio	77.8%	47.6%
Press	56.1	83.2
Television	33.8	34.3
N =	1,340	688
(Chi square = 112.4, p is less than .01)		

SOURCE: Letic [1977], p. 52.
NOTE: The data for Croatia reflect those who said they used specific media only for information or for information and amusement.

In addition, based on an agreement between the Yugoslavs and their foreign partners, a large number of stations in Europe have regular programs for the Yugoslav workers. These are usually produced in Yugoslavia as "a program for abroad under the auspices of the Radio Zagreb Correspondence Center" "in direct cooperation with the remaining republic and province radio stations." Among the stations broadcasting programs targeted to the Yugoslav workers are Radio Cologne, Radio Frankfurt, Radio Free Berlin, Radio Zurich, Radio Vienna, Radio Paris, Radio Liège, Radio Luxembourg, Radio Hilversum (The Netherlands), and Radio Stockholm [Letic, 1977, p. 18].

Television plays some part in linking the workers abroad to Yugoslavia, though its role is considerably more modest than that of radio for several reasons. [For a complaint that it is underutilized, see Kozina in OECD, *Joint Project*, 1975, p. 74.] Relatively few workers abroad have television sets. In the mid-1970s, workers abroad from Croatia had basically the same number of radios as did their counterparts in Croatia (77 per cent vs. 73 per cent); but only 38 per cent had television, in comparison with 53 per cent at home [Letic, 1977, p. 37]. Most programs apparently are blends of materials prepared by Zagreb Television "in cooperation with the remaining republic and provincial TV centers" [Letic, 1977, p. 18], and the relevant European stations. With respect to the notion of governing the workers abroad, what is perhaps most interesting is that "Good Morning Yugoslavia," which is broadcast on the German Second Television Program, is prepared "ready made" by Zagreb Television [Kozina in OECD, *Joint Project*, 1975, p. 71].

At the same time, the fact that these programs are conducted through German or Swedish TV necessarily constrains their content, even when they are produced by Yugoslavs in, for instance, Zagreb, since the arrangement is conditioned on the absence of materials of a "political nature" [Letic, 1977, p. 106].

Numerous Yugoslav papers are also widely available in Western Europe. Throughout the 1970s, *Vjesnik u srijedu* published a "green supplement" on a weekly basis that ran to between 20,000 and 40,000 copies. Daily newspapers put out special issues for workers. One source reports official figures that claim that "25 million issues of various newspapers, of which about 40 per cent are political-informative," targeted to the workers abroad appeared in the year 1975 [Letic, 1977, p. 17].

For our purposes, however, the most noteworthy item relating to Yugoslav newspapers concerns *Vjesnik*, the major Zagreb newspaper, and *Oslobodjenje* (Sarajevo). From late 1974 on, *Vjesnik* has published—in Frankfurt—a daily edition for Yugoslav migrants throughout Europe. So, too, does *Oslobodjenje*. The press run of *Vjesnik* in Frankfurt is a rather modest 5,000 to 10,000 copies, but from the perspective of international-national linkages, the significance is not. For here we have highly authoritative Yugoslav newspapers not merely available outside the *de jure* borders of Yugoslavia, but actually published there.

The impression that it is a false dichotomy to think of Yugoslav workers as being either abroad or at home is further strengthened when we focus on the socialization and education of the children of workers abroad, rather than on the workers themselves. Here, too, as in so many other instances, the evidence of the Yugoslav authorities' systematic concern for the children of workers abroad dates from 1970; however, the concern was not fully expressed until the mid-1970s. By the 1980s, the education of the children of Yugoslav workers abroad had become a substantial phenomenon. In 1981-1982, almost 81,000 Yugoslav children were attending compulsory schools in Western Europe. Of those, roughly two-thirds were receiving supplementary instruction in courses dealing with Yugoslav geography, history, and culture. As befits a multinational state, instruction in these subjects takes place in eight of the languages of Yugoslavia, ranging from Serbo-Croatian, Slovenian, Macedonian, and Albanian to Hungarian, Turkish, Romanian, and Slovak. The textbooks employed are those used in schools in Yugoslavia, plus a book targeted specifically to the children of workers abroad, *Moja domovina—SFR Jugoslavija* (*Yugoslavia—My Homeland*) [OECD, 1982, p. 205]. The theme of governing the seventh republic in ways highly congruent with the governing of the other republics is italicized by the fact that the education and schooling of the children of the workers abroad is the responsibility (based on a 1980 Social Agreement) of the republics. It is they that "provide financial resources for the work of teachers, take care of the selection and preparation of the teachers, send textbooks and other teaching aids necessary for supplementary education abroad'' [OECD, 1982, p. 207] with coordination being accomplished in Belgrade by a commission specifically charged to monitor the schooling of Yugoslav citizens abroad.

Such schooling may take place either in the regular school curriculum, as an adjunct to that curriculum, or be completely divorced from it. Likewise, the teachers may be Yugoslavs recruited abroad or be persons sent from Yugoslavia specifically for the purpose. Generally, when the instruction is an integral part of the regular curriculum, replacing some other subject, the host country bears the costs. The most common practice is that the courses are taught as supplements to the regular lessons after school. In these circumstances, the host country and the Yugoslav authorities cofinance the instruction. Finally, such schooling may take place outside the regular public school curriculum entirely—on Saturdays, generally. When this occurs, the financing derives almost entirely from Yugoslav sources. It is, of course, the last of these three that is most in keeping with the theme of direct governance by Yugoslavia of its seventh republic. Similarly, the recruitment of teachers directly from Yugoslavia most bespeaks the treatment of the workers abroad as part of a putative seventh republic. Of the 974 teachers who taught Yugoslav children in Western Europe during 1981-1982, 636 were drawn from Yugoslavs abroad, and 338 were sent from Yugoslavia (see Table 5.8).

Interestingly, it is in Germany—where the overwhelming number of Yugoslav workers are—France, and Austria that we find the highest proportion of instructors in Yugoslav languages that actually come from Yugoslavia. In those countries, we witness teachers from Yugoslavia, selected by Yugoslav local and republic bodies, teaching children of Yugoslavs subjects conventional to the civic training of Yugoslav citizens in much the same way as occurs in Yugoslavia's (other) six republics.

TABLE 5.8
Teachers of Yugoslav Origin in Western Europe, 1980-1981

Country	Yugoslav Teachers from Yugoslavia	Employed from Host Country
Germany	252	166
France	35	25
Austria	36	20
Sweden	0	275
Switzerland	3	73
The Netherlands	1	46
Other European States	11	31
Total	338	636

SOURCE: OECD [1982], p. 206.

Analogous patterns are discernible in the area of social welfare. Needless to say, the bulk of Yugoslav efforts to ensure that the workers abroad enjoy social welfare benefits has focused on bilateral or multilateral (through the International Labor Organization, most notably) negotiations with the host countries. There are, in addition, direct contacts with the trade unions of the relevant countries, and in several instances, the Savez sindikata Jugoslavija (Yugoslav Federation of Trade Unions) has permanent representatives attached to the host country trade unions. Moreover, "social workers from Yugoslavia are regularly employed in social institutions in regions [in Western Europe] where there is a large concentration of Yugoslav workers" [Baucic, 1975, p. 25]. Even more notably, the German institution Arbeiterwohlfahrt and the French agency for migrant workers APTM, "employ social workers sent abroad by official Yugoslav institutions." In the mid-1970s, for instance, 110 social workers sent from Yugoslavia were employed by the German agency, and APTM had "three posts for social workers" sent by the Yugoslav Federal Bureau for Employment Affairs. As in the selection of social workers within Yugoslavia, the Yugoslav authorities insist that the social workers sent to Western Europe be both expert and red—that they are "not only properly qualified, but that they also possess the moral qualities necessary for this kind of work" [Baucic, 1975, p. 25]. Indeed, Baucic provides a glimmer of the way nationality tensions carry over into the seventh republic: Yugoslavs, he urges, "must also try to ensure that the national composition of social workers corresponds to the national composition of Yugoslav migrants in the region of their work" [Baucic, 1975, p. 25]—by which he surely means, "Don't send speakers of the Serbian variant to work among the Croatian *gastarbeiter* in Germany." In like fashion, the German charitable organizations Caritas and Diakonisches Werk employ social workers who come from Yugoslavia, and the Yugoslav Catholic and Orthodox Churches have priests all over Europe who provide "social assistance" [Baucic, 1975, p. 26]. (Mark Baskin's dissertation [Michigan, 1986] argues that a major driving concern of the Yugoslav authorities that prompted them to send social workers was that the Yugoslav churches—the Catholic Church especially—were reaching Yugoslavs abroad while providing social welfare services.)

In short, the picture that emerges of the handling of the Yugoslav workers abroad by the Yugoslav authorities is one that has some real parallels with regime-mass relations in the six Yugoslav republics. While the point can be overdrawn, it remains the case that Yugoslav citizens who commit acts outside Yugoslavia that are illegal in Yugoslavia are arrested and incarcerated when they come within the reach of the Yugoslav police. There appear also to have been instances where the Yugoslav secret police have acted against Yugoslavs outside Yugoslavia. Radio and TV programs produced in Zagreb are heard and/or seen in Western Europe and Yugoslav newspapers are dis-seminated—and in the case of *Vjesnik* and *Oslobodjenje*—even produced outside the formal borders of Yugoslavia. Yugoslav teachers in Western Europe teach Yugoslav students, in the languages of Yugoslavia, courses about Yugoslavia—and social workers sent from Yugoslavia handle welfare cases of Yugoslav citizens.

The next section of this chapter considers the implications of the seventh republic and its governance for regime-society relations in the remaining six republics.

THE SEVENTH REPUBLIC AND THE POLITICAL CONSEQUENCES OF OPENNESS

That issue may be addressed in several ways. One task is to explore the ways the workers abroad have themselves become a political issue. A second is to specify the ways the existence of the seventh republic constrains and influences the policy choices of the Yugoslav leadership. A third is to ask how regime-society relations in Yugoslavia would differ from the present situation if there were no open borders policy or if there were a fundamental shift in that policy.

Where there are policy options there are politics. What to do about the borders and the workers abroad has been a subject of high-level sniping from various sides for years. There is a view that surfaces periodically which may be characterized as old left—"Cominformist," in Yugoslav parlance. The basis for such a view is fairly straightforward. For reasons adumbrated above, being linked to the international market is considered a dangerous and harmful policy—dangerous because of the likelihood of a European or German economic crisis; harmful because it places Yugoslavia in a neo-colonialist position vis-à-vis (German) imperialism, and strengthens the restoration of capitalism within Yugoslavia. The attendant acceleration of social stratification is not dismissed as "inevitable in the present historical period"; efficiency is to be traded off for a more egalitarian social structure. The individual who migrates, in this view, especially if he has specialized skills, is virtually disloyal, and at a minimum should offset the cost of his training by depositing some kind of bond equivalent to the amount paid for his education prior to his departure abroad. This particular idea has surfaced relatively infrequently, in part because it so obviously smacks of a Soviet-style exit policy [but see *Borba*, April 8, 1971, and *NIN*, October 8, 1972]. For the nation, migration constitutes a form of selling Yugoslav workers to foreign capitalists; rather than such a tack, the regime should assure employment within the country for all. The broader attitudes this orientation reflects find wide resonance in Yugoslavia, even for those who are unwilling to pay the political price that a commitment to domestic full employment currently involves. This should be scarcely surprising in a country where the political culture is permeated with egalitarianism. The resentment toward the workers who had gone abroad found expression in a kind of rear-guard action at the enterprise level against the federally sanctioned policy of openness. Baucic [1978, p. 12] reports that it required the "intervention of the socio-political organizations" to overturn the statutes of enterprises which "as late as 1972" still had rules that thwarted the rehiring of workers who had left jobs to go abroad to work. At the leadership level, the attitudes illustrated by the behavior of some enterprises have found greatest resonance among the trade-union leadership and the military. They have been an often-struck but minor chord for two decades, always yielding to the dominant themes of the desirability of openness and the reality of hard currency remittances.

The occasion during which the workers abroad were of greatest salience as a political issue was the 1971 upsurge of Croatian nationalism. At that time the workers became a focal point of highly conflictual politics, the overall theme of which was that Croatia was being exploited by the federation, by Belgrade, by the banks, and by the Serbs. With respect to the migrant workers per se, the issue was the tie between migration and the long-term relations between Croatia and the rest of the country. Members of the Croatian LCY leadership took the stance that a reversal in migration trends was a condition for good relations between Croatia and the Federation. Thus, Dragutin Haramija, then president of the Croatian Executive Council, said: "I must frankly say no federal government which in the period to come would consider the possibility of even more of our citizens departing for abroad and relying on their checks to solve Yugoslavia's balance of payments problem could expect support from Croatia" [*Politika*, April 8, 1971]. Other Croats viewed the matter in more strident terms: for them, "exploitation" understated the matter. Instead, they saw a more sinister design wherein the intention was to reduce the number of Croats and the influence of Croatia within Yugoslavia [Komarica, 1970; Djodan, 1969, pp. 31-49]. Within this group, one element adopted the stance that the "autonomous position (*samostalniji polozaj*) of Croatia within the federation of the peoples of Yugoslavia" would create conditions wherein Croatia could deal quickly and adequately with its overall population problems, including the regulation of its workers wishing to migrate abroad; and that, to quote the conclusions of a study of the Croatian Pugwash Group (*sic*), measures in the regions of migration, employment, and population "are an inseparable part of the sovereignty of the Republic, the working class, and the people of SR Croatia" [*Encyclopedia moderna*, Winter 1971, p. 107].

During the late 1980s, views that one republic or one ethnic group is being exploited, or even decimated by the workers' migration abroad, are likely to surface once again. This time, however, as the analysis in Chapter 4 suggested, the putative victims are likely to be Serbia and the Serbs; already the outmigration of Serbs from Kosovo to Serbia proper is a burning symbolic issue. A likely trend is that this issue, the issue of Serbian migration abroad, and that of the relative weight of Serbia in Yugoslavia will merge and become highly salient politically at some juncture in the late 1980s.

The *gastarbeiter* have been an issue of politics during the years since the Croatian mass movement and the 1971 Zagreb student strike in a considerably less dramatic way; for the most part, the issue has not been a matter of high politics; rather, it has been manifest largely at the commune or even the enterprise level. We have already described an instance in 1972 when the government intervened to prevent enterprises from impeding the re-employment of workers who had gone abroad: resistance then was sufficiently strong that *Ekonomska politika* [January 24, 1972, p. 4] observed:

> An ordinary man whose work is paid in ordinary dinars will probably wonder what has induced a TU official to show a special concern about our people whose work is paid in marks or francs. . . . These people have availed themselves of the freedom to choose their job in a way which they considered best. . . .
>
> The trade unions and others should be more concerned . . . for those hundreds of thousands of men seeking employment in the country.
>
> . . . Taking into account knowledge and experience acquired in industrialized Europe, every returned worker will have . . . a great advantage over every domestic competitor leaving his village to seek employment in a town.

The implication that returning workers, by virtue of their return, might deny others jobs became even more apparent later in the 1970s as unemployment grew. Resistance to the declaratory policy of encouraging the reintegration of returning workers was widespread. Baucic [1978, p. 13] summarizes the situation thus: the policy "did not receive adequate support from quite a number of socio-political and administrative structures. The implementation of this policy was especially slow in the relevant civil services."

We noted in the introduction that traditionally, communist systems have been characterized by low trust in the citizenry by the leadership. That lack of trust—archetypically exemplified in Lenin's suspicion of spontaneity—found expression in the basic policies of the early post-World War II Yugoslav communist state. Yugoslavia, like other communist countries, was a closed political system, one which endeavored to insulate the citizenry from outside influences, and endeavored also to insulate the regime from constraints on its behavior by the citizenry. From that perspective, surely the most significant result of opening the borders and the massive outpouring of Yugoslav workers for stays of substantial duration in Europe and elsewhere was the absence of any drastic antiregime behavior by those who went abroad. Neither in the mid-1960s, when the policy was initiated, nor in 1970-1971, during the peak of the Croatian national movement, were there dramatic antiregime manifestations by those who had gone abroad. Moreover, as we have seen, while attitudes among those who have spent considerable time abroad differ from those who have not, such evidence as there is suggests that identification with the homeland does not diminish substantially. (Whether the homeland is Slovenia, Croatia, or Serbia, as the case may be, or Yugoslavia, is another matter.) This has contributed substantially to the official legitimacy accorded the Yugoslav self-definition—both at the leadership level and among the politically aware—as an open country. (The preamble to the 1974 Yugoslav Constitution explicitly declares that Yugoslavia is "an open community"; see also Micovic's significantly titled *The Openness of Yugoslavia before the World: Concerning the Freedom of Exchange of Information and Cultural Goods and the Movement of People"* [1977].) How seriously Yugoslavs take that conception has been most vividly exemplified in recent years by the profound resentment produced by the introduction, in 1982, ostensibly for economic reasons, of the "deposit" required of Yugoslavs going abroad for nonbusiness reasons, and in the rapidity with which the deposit was subsequently abandoned. It also found public expression earlier in the resistance articulated to proposals advanced in the early 1970s that would have required migrant workers to have the right political attitudes as a condition for being allowed to go abroad to work.

At the time, March 1973, when major measures were being adopted to regulate the outflow of workers, it will be recalled that Tito had already successfully purged the Croatian and Serbian republic party organizations. It was a time, too, when Tito's "Letter" was defining the overall political agenda; when the refrains of democratic centralism and the guiding role of the party were being heard with great frequency. Even in that setting, however, proposals that would fundamentally circumscribe the right to exit were rejected out of hand, for instance, by *Politika*. It thundered that such proposals raised the prospects of a reversion "to times when the obtaining of passports depended on janitors' statements" and to "the system of political absolutism," as well as held out the prospect that "members of the League of Communists would have priority with regard to work in capitalist enterprises" [*Politika*, March 18, 1973].

Moreover, even if we assume a Yugoslavia where the prevailing members of the elite are disposed to return to a closed society, the workers abroad represent a fundamental constraint on such an option. We have become accustomed to communist systems using their citizens as hostages to ensure the good behavior of citizens allowed to go abroad. The seventh republic in important ways constrains the regime's alternatives. We have already noted how attentive the leadership is to ensuring the continued flow of remittances from abroad; deliberate acts that would interrupt that flow are practically inconceivable. (In a rather analogous instance in Portugal, the prospect of a drastic reduction in remittances played a key role in shaping the outcome of that country's political crisis in the mid-1970s.) In addition, it turns out that the workers abroad have created a situation within Yugoslavia that severely constrains the choices of the political leadership. As a result of the remittances, individual citizens in the six republics dispose of virtually all the country's hard currency. By the mid-1970s, more than 1.75 million hard currency accounts had been established in Yugoslav banks, and "82 per cent of the entire convertible currency and gold reserves" were in private hands [Tadic, 1975, p. 34].

In addition, the facts that a sizable fraction of the citizenry spends an important part of their early adult years abroad, and that basically all Yugoslavs can leave the country, have profound implications for the socialization process and media control in Yugoslavia. While there are deterrents to the availability of Western materials in Yugoslavia, the open borders policy links Yugoslav mass culture with Western mass culture in ways that distinguish Yugoslavia rather dramatically from a more modal communist system.

At the same time, the existence of the seventh republic has important consequences for the Yugoslav political economy. If we recall the original economic motives that prompted the decision to open the borders—those associated with the 1965 economic reform—there can be little doubt that the market for labor outside the country has absorbed enormous numbers of Yugoslavs who would otherwise have been unemployed. As a consequence, it has been correspondingly easier to justify market socialism which, despite the many political factories, inevitably results in far greater unemployment than "state socialism." The hard currency remittances also facilitate to some degree other market-socialist goals—modernization of plant and quasi-convertibility—and in important ways link the Yugoslav economy to the international economy.

There are other consequences as well. For one thing, the existence of the seventh republic exacerbates the already well-developed revolution of rising expectations among Yugoslavs. Crucial as the remissions are to the Yugoslav economy, it must, nevertheless, be recognized that the demand for West European products is also greatly enhanced by time abroad, and that conspicuous consumption is a characteristic feature of the guest workers' expenditure patterns. These range from expensive and overly large houses to color television sets in villages still devoid of electricity, and enormous family grave sites.

Ironically, moreover, some of the impetus to conspicuous consumption comes from ideologically grounded impediments to investment: lacking a socialist stock market, particularly given the constraints on agricultural landholding, there is little incentive to invest except in consumer durables. Compounding matters, the inflation rate throughout the 1970s was well above the interest rate; as a result, it was foolish not to acquire consumer durables, a vacation property [*vikenditsa*], and the like. The immigration phenomenon also increased the stratification of Yugoslav society. Those with skills can readily double, and in many instances, quadruple their salaries abroad, and the skilled are to be found disproportionately in Yugoslavia's northern republics. Even the unskilled abroad, moreover, earn far more than their counterparts at home. As a result, the existence of the seventh republic aggravates the already-substantial stratification of Yugoslav society geographically, between the skilled and the unskilled, and between those who have been abroad and those who have not. That stratification is exacerbated, moreover, both directly, by virtue of the earnings of the workers, and indirectly as a result of market responses to deter the skilled from going abroad. The inequalities take the form not only of wage differentials. In addition, differential access to hard currency allows one group access to better and/or more desirable goods—goods that, moreover, tend to be flaunted in a society as oriented to consumerism as is Yugoslavia. In short, not only does the existence of the seventh republic have redistributive consequences, it amplifies already existing propensities for those consequences to be highly visible.

It also contributes to the development of the modest Yugoslav service sector. There is something fittingly ironic about a picture of Yugoslav workers and peasants going off to work for four to seven years in capitalist Western Europe and returning to jobs which Marxists would label petit bourgeois—as the tourist industry, for instance, grows, and as Yugoslav *gastarbeiter* return to become restaurant owners, taxi drivers, and the like. The data, such as they are, do not support the notion that this is a widespread phenomenon. By and large, the number employed in "the social sector" before departure and on return remains constant: in one 1977 survey, 41.8 per cent of the sample had been employed in the social sector prior to departure, and 40.4 per cent were so employed on their return [Nejasmic, 1981, p. 60].

The trend is, however, there. Only slightly more than one-third of the returnees return to the same place of work. The one sectoral area where more than half (indeed 62.5 per cent) do return to the same place is the broad rubric of restaurant and hotel operation [Nejasmic, 1981, p. 68]. A shift in the employment patterns within the social sector also occurs in the direction of the tertiary sector, as Table 5.9 reveals.

Additionally, there is a sizable increase among the returnees—against a low base—in the number who are self-employed as restaurateurs or craftsmen: whereas 1.6 per cent were self-supporting craftsmen and shop owners prior to departure, more than three times as many (5.8 per cent of the total) were such on their return [Nejasmic, 1981, pp. 60, 62]. In short, while it is an overgeneralization to view the existence of the seventh republic as leading to Yugoslavia becoming a nation of shopkeepers, this seventh republic does contribute to the growth of a socialist petit bourgeoisie and to the growth of the service sector.

There is an additional consideration relating to mass-regime relations in Yugoslavia stemming from the fact that the workers abroad were there for a considerable period (*not* temporarily) and that the outmigration phenomenon had become an essentially permanent, not short-term, fixture for Yugoslavia. In the 1960s, the external world had been the escape mechanism whereby unemployment had been kept relatively modest despite the economic reforms. In the 1970s, in the aftermath of the upsurge of unemployment in Europe following the 1973 OPEC oil-price rise, the number of workers returning to Yugoslavia exceeded the number departing by 135,000 in the three years 1974 to 1976 [Nejasmic, 1981, p. 16]. Partly as a consequence, the number of unemployed in Yugoslavia increased by 198,000 from October 1974 to October 1976, even though the total number employed also increased in the same period from 4.63 million to nearly 5.04 million [*Indeks*, December 1976, p. 39]. This development almost certainly had an impact on attitudes toward economic interdependence as an overall development strategy, and its implicit Western orientation of the economy.

Tito gave his "three missing armies" speech in November 1972, and major changes in the rules related to migration were adopted in March 1973. Even against this background, it would be difficult to assert that the jump in European unemployment and the subsequent increase in the return rates of

TABLE 5.9
Employment by Economic Sector

Economic Sector	Before Departure	After return
I. Agriculture, fishing, and hunting	5.7	3.0
II. Mining, industry, construction, manufacturing	52.0	50.9
III. Remaining activities	42.3	46.1
	100.0	100.0

SOURCE: Nejasmic [1981], p. 70.

Yugoslavs had an impact on regime-society relations in Yugoslavia any-where comparable to the initial decision to open the country's borders, or the way regime policy options were constrained by the fact that Yugo-slavia's dependence on remittances rendered the balance of payments deficit at least modestly manageable, or by the concentration of hard currency in private hands.

This observation also implies an answer to the third question raised at the beginning of this section: how would regime-society relations differ if there were no open borders policy, or if there were a truly significant shift in that policy? This, in turn, takes us back to Hirschman's point about exit, and enhances our appreciation of the political consequences of openness: the concept of the mobilization system has been central to our notion of regime-society relations in communist states. It is possible that the Yugoslav polit-ical system would have evolved, in any event, in a way quite differently from the Soviet model as symbols such as federalism, market socialism, and self-management took on institutional form—each, if genuine, implies the devolution of power respectively to republics, the market, and the workers. What seems manifestly clear, however, is that a policy of openness to the international system has important consequences for the political system. It alters the distribution of power in a state between the regime and the society in ways that virtually preclude mobilization as a strategy. In the absence of voice as expressed in choices among competing elites, exit serves quite ef-fectively to constrain the political elite while simultaneously increasing cit-izen loyalty.

6

CONCLUSION:
INTERNATIONAL-NATIONAL LINKAGES AND THE
POLITICAL EVOLUTION OF YUGOSLAVIA

This study has taken, as it were, three "cuts" at the subject of the interaction of the evolution of the Yugoslav political system and Yugoslavia's international environment. One was at the level of the state itself and pertained primarily to the leadership's evolving strategies for ensuring the independence of multinational socialist Yugoslavia in a world of states. The second cut illustrated the way external actors and external resources are coupled to political processes in Yugoslavia and influence the evolution of Yugoslav political institutions in ways that structure the game of politics in Yugoslavia. The third level of analysis was that of the relation between Yugoslavia's links to the international environment and the evolution of the relation between regime and society in Yugoslavia.

The first cut depicted Yugoslavia's interactions with its international environment at the level of the state and the leadership's international security strategies and concentrated on Yugoslav alignment policies. In one sense, consequently, that analysis could be thought of as simply a conventional essay on Yugoslav foreign policy. Even from that perspective, there are interesting and important trends to be discerned. Initially the foreign policy of the "new," post-World War II Yugoslavia was one of conscious alignment with the Soviet Union and the other Peoples' Democracies. "Conscious" and "alignment" are each equally important elements in that statement. In foreign policy as elsewhere, Tito's Yugoslavia between 1945 and 1948 demonstrated its autonomy from the U.S.S.R. as much by its zealousness in carrying out pro-Soviet policies as it did by pursuing policies that meshed with the particularist interests of Yugoslavia.

The Cominform attack on Tito in 1948 put an abrupt end to Yugoslavia's alignment with the Soviet Union. Forced to choose between alignment and national independence, Tito and most of the Yugoslav leadership and most of the Yugoslav citizenry opted for independence. That independence did not translate immediately into nonalignment. For a short while Yugoslavia stood isolated from all the great powers. There followed a period, almost as brief, in which Yugoslavia seemed to verge on alignment with the U.S. After Stalin's death, the rise of Nikita Khrushchev in the Soviet Union, and the ouster of Milovan Djilas in Yugoslavia, there followed yet another brief period in which a special relationship developed between the U.S.S.R. and Yugoslavia, a relationship that terminated abruptly with the Soviet invasion of Hungary in November 1956. Henceforth, nonalignment would be the key to Yugoslav foreign policy. From 1949 to 1956, however, the outlines of what would constitute the content of nonalignment in the Tito era became evident. There was first the turn to the global south and away from either the East or the West. A second major component of the nascent nonalignment policy was the globalist, rather than regional, quality of Tito's foreign policy. To these strands, which date to the immediate post-Cominform resolution years, other elements were added as nonalignment emerged as a fully articulated policy. One was the commitment (more honored in the breach than in practice) to a balanced trade with the global east, west, and south. Another was the strategy of the general people's defense, the declaratory position of which is a military strategy of self-reliance premised on the possibility of attack from those who would destroy the self-managing or socialist character of Yugoslavia—although its emergence as a full-blown doctrine in the aftermath of the Soviet invasion of Czechoslovakia indicated that the awareness of the Soviet danger was the immediate catalyst for the doctrine.

Since Tito's death in 1980, we have witnessed the emergence of a more regional cast to nonalignment and a rationale for the policy that was explicitly and specifically justified by pragmatic concerns rather than on ideological grounds. Thus, if we look for the foreign policy bases of Yugoslavia's nonaligned policy in the 1980s, we would focus primarily on two areas. One is the benefits that accrue from occupying a strategic position between the blocs, the other is the economic gains from trading with the global west, south and east. To pay for its imports, Yugoslavia must export goods and labor to Europe and the United States; to cope with its energy deficiency, it must export to the Soviet Union and to the global south. From a foreign policy perspective per se, aspirations to cast Yugoslavia in the remainder of the 1980s as a global political leader of the nonaligned are likely to get rather short shrift. Much more typical in the 1980s will be views—whether justified by invoking Tito's name or no—such as those recently articulated by Lazar Mojsov, former Secretary for Foreign Affairs and in 1984 a member of the Yugoslav State Presidency: "Tito," Mojsov told readers of the *Review of International Affairs*, "gave precedence to bilateral initiatives and talks or talks within regional organizations as peaceful means for solving disputes between nonaligned countries" [*Tanjug*, May 22, 1984, in *FBIS*, May 23, 1984, p. I 6].

While there are important trends to note in the evolution of Yugoslav behavior in the international environment, for our purposes what is more central is the link between Yugoslavia's changed international environment and the evolution of the defining features of Yugoslav socialism. As Alvin Rubinstein first observed, nonalignment has the attractive feature that it is minimally acceptable to all the members of the domestic coalition. The argument developed in Chapter 2 extends that proposition. I argue that there are important dimensions to an understanding of Yugoslavia's nonalignment policy that transcend conclusions which emerge either from thinking of nonalignment merely as a product of Yugoslavia's existence in a world of states, or as an outgrowth of domestic politics. Rather, the commitment doctrinally to self-management as a defining attribute of Yugoslav socialism was an outgrowth of the foreign policy trends that came to be known as non-alignment. To play a global role and to differentiate Yugoslavia from the U.S.S.R. and the U.S. implied nonalignment. Nonalignment, in turn, in the Yugoslav doctrinal context, implied self-managing socialism. Moreover, the Yugoslavs quickly learned that occupying a saddle point between the two blocs was not only excellent from a strategic perspective, but also from the vantage point of internal developmental goals and needs. It demonstrated strikingly that external political penetration, if that penetration stems from plural sources, can actually strengthen a government and enhance its ability to implement its domestic political agenda. That strategy for internal development continued throughout the first years of the post-Tito period, despite the accumulation of a massive internal debt and renewed imprecations from many quarters in Yugoslavia and abroad about the IMF, "the debt trap," and the dangers of (inter)dependence.

The second "cut" at assessing international-national linkages in Yugoslavia was directed at the evolution of Yugoslav political institutions and processes. Chapter 3 described the Yugoslav elite's evolving strategy for assuring national cohesion and also related the way events in the international environment influence Yugoslav policy processes. These two phenomena are interconnected. The institutional setting for the game of politics has reflected the evolution in Yugoslav elite thinking concerning the most appropriate means for ensuring national cohesion; the experience of particular episodes, in turn, also demonstrably affected the evolution of Yugoslav elite thought.

The institutional evolution of Yugoslavia in the period since World War II may be readily summarized. With some qualifications, the story is one in which the Yugoslavs emulated the Soviet pattern of power seizure and then set out with a vengeance in the immediate postwar period to emulate the Soviet Union. Thus, the Yugoslavs came to power more or less on their own; they created a monolithic party organization, the operative guidelines for which were democratic centralism as that concept has been traditionally understood in the U.S.S.R.; copied the Soviet "Stalin" constitution; adopted a command economy and five-year plans; monopolized foreign trade; and closed the borders. The Leninist model was also crucial in making it possible for Tito to resist Stalin successfully in 1948. The kind of penetration of the party, government, the instruments of coercion, and the economy that the U.S.S.R. achieved in the other Peoples' Democracies of Eastern Europe proved impossible to achieve in Yugoslavia. Leninism is, in a sense, a strategy of national independence and its institutional forms facilitate the efforts of small states to resist pressures short of war by imperial powers, even when that imperial power is itself a state organized on a Leninist model.

After the Cominform-Yugoslav clash, however, the proposition that the institutionalized Leninist party was the most effective organizational strategy for ensuring national cohesion in the face of external threat (along with, in the Yugoslav context, domestically driven fissiparous tendencies) began to be rethought. Dating from the early 1950s there evolved a more consensual and less mobilizational strategy in relation to society. The pervasive role of the central party leadership also attenuated. Institutionally, power devolved from the central party leadership to the republics and to the government as the system changed in the direction of a genuinely federal system and as formal state institutions took on substantial roles. Simultaneously, the autonomous provinces of Kosovo and Vojvodina and their respective party organizations increasingly acquired perquisites and privileges blurring the distinctions between them and the six republics. At the level of the Federation, the institutions of the party were changed: democratic centralism was defined more loosely, the previously all-encompassing ambit of the Executive Committee (Politburo) was limited and, in 1970, Tito decided to establish a State Presidency, the leadership of which, after Tito's death, would rotate automatically.

The 1969 Slovenian road affair, and the nationalist upsurge in Croatia in 1970-1971—both of which were events with strong international-national linkage dimensions—served as a backdrop for a return to Leninist symbols in the early 1970s. For several years after the publication of Tito's "Letter" in 1972, it seemed that Tito intended to revert to the Leninist party structures that had allowed the partisans to seize power and facilitated Yugoslavia's resistance to Stalin in 1948. Certainly all the traditional Leninist symbols were reaffirmed: democratic centralism and the dictatorship of the proletariat were stressed, cadre issues were emphasized, the State Presidency downgraded, the republic party leaderships purged, and the party Presidium strengthened in ways that suggested the re-establishment of an institution playing the role of a traditional Leninist politburo.

In the mid-1980s, however, these changes now appear far less consequential than they seemed at the time. The republic party organizations remained powerful. Consensual decisionmaking remained the practice and

135

"harmonization" of positions the norm. While Tito lived, the democratic dimensions of democratic centralism were accented: at the Eleventh Congress in 1978 the LCY rules were altered to allow persons to retain their positions when in the minority. In addition, republic and provincial party organizations were described as having "equal responsibility" with central party organs. After Tito, consensus continued manifestly to serve as the guiding principle for relations among the republic party organizations and between the republic organizations and the Federation. It was a strange Leninist model in which a key political figure could describe unanimity of a decision as "the highest form of democratic centralism." Indeed, in practice much of the re-Leninization of the party that occurred in the 1970s transpired more at the republic and commune level than at the center.

At the level of the Federation, moreover, the renewed attention to Leninist symbols was paralleled by a concomitant attention to harmonization and decentralization. An institutional setting which stressed parity among the six republics (or the eight republics and provinces) and elite consensus was encouraged by the 1974 Constitution. Such institutional developments as transpired in the period after the 1969 Slovenian road affair and the 1971 Croatian crisis seemed designed to encourage a policy process that corresponded nicely to Theodore Lowi's arena of distribution, an arena characterized by logrolling, unprincipled alliances, and low conflict among elites. To be avoided at great cost were the more conflictual arenas of power—regulation and redistribution. (The former is typified by pluralistic and multi-centered coalitions of like-minded groups; the latter is a highly conflictual arena of power where large social aggregates—movements, classes, or generations—occupy center stage.)

The political arrangement termed here "consociational authoritarianism" involved a blend of a return to Leninist symbols and policies on the one hand, and an emphasis on consensus among the republics—harmonization—on the other. It was a political formula played out in different ways at two levels of Yugoslav politics in the last years of Tito's life and in the early post-Tito period. In the early post-Tito period (and in the period immediately prior to Tito's death when he played a quite limited role), *inter*-republic politics may be described as becoming increasingly consociational. Within the Republic of Serbia, by contrast, the tendency since Tito's death has been to reverse the trend of the entire Tito period and to differentiate the provinces from the republics. Instead, on issue after issue, the proposition that the competence of the republic party and state organs embraces the entire territory of SR Serbia has been asserted.

We now know that all these fundamentally redistributive issues were part of the agenda of politics from 1977 on, but the existence of these disputes was a closely held secret until 1981. The 1981 riots in Kosovo brought these

136

issues out into the open and resulted in the kinds of policy processes be-tween elites and elites associated with redistributive politics. As in Zagreb in 1971 (and Kosovo in 1968), 1981 in Kosovo witnessed ethnically de-fined, highly mobilized, and highly conflictual mass politics and counter-elites asserting significant symbolic claims. These claims usually related to republic status for Kosovo, though they were sometimes explicitly seces-sionary. Following the imposition of near-martial law in Kosovo, Serbia continued to pursue policies that stress that symbolically and jurisdiction-ally, Kosovo—and Vojvodina as well—are part of SR Serbia. The intent, patently, is to keep the Albanians in their place and to assert that republic status for Kosovo would result inevitably in secession and the dissolution of Yugoslavia.

With respect to the game of politics at the level of the Federation, con-sociational authoritarianism has had greater success. Nevertheless, the game of politics has evolved in ways that are incompatible with a strategy for ensuring cohesion by cutting in the elites from each republic on the basis of some principle of shares (six-sixths, etc.). That strategy has run afoul of severe resource constraints. They are, in turn, a function of Yugoslavia's $20 billion external debt. Pork barrel politics and logrolling are less feasible options when the political resource "pie" is constant, or contracting, than when it is expanding. Faced with the task of making hard decisions, the Yu-goslavs developed two characteristic policy processes. In October 1982 when things became really bad, that kind of crisis atmosphere produced the minimally conflictual policies one expects in crises. Jure Bilic's 1983 New Year's remark cited previously that "Unity is created in party leaderships . . . when it is a matter of do or die" is an observation about crisis politics that is neither time- nor system-specific.

On numerous other occasions since 1979, many clearly entailing mani-fest international-national linkages, the Yugoslavs have experienced far more conflictual politics—but absent the mass mobilization of redistributive politics. Rather, these decisions have been more like the patterns associated with Lowi's arena of regulation, i.e., a process characterized by conflict be-tween coalitions of interest groups. In these instances, consensus and the effort to avoid conflict as a systematic strategy have had to defer to the need to govern in response to the acute need to decide how to link with the global economy. The only two issues between 1969 and 1971 occurring within a republic which became agenda items for the central party leadership were the Slovenian road affair and the Croatian mass movement. The first in-stance, when the FEC resorted to the mechanisms that allow governance in the absence of consensus as provided in the 1974 Constitution, involved the balance of payments. Immense controversy in the early 1980s, as in 1971, has again attended the rules relating to rights of enterprises to retain foreign currency. The requirement imposed in 1982 that Yugoslavs leave a deposit prior to traveling abroad was the subject of especially intense political pressure.

In an economy of scarcity, except during periods of genuine crisis, harmonization and politics as usual are likely to give way to the hard choices and zero-sum politics of the arena of regulation. Whether it will be possible to contain such conflict depends on many things—including the recovery of a global economy, the extent the hard choices are perceived as apolitical, whether the coalitions are crosscutting and shifting or unidirectional and constant. To the Yugoslavs' credit, however, they had developed institutions in the 1970s that presumed interethnic elite consensus but that made provision for governance absent that consensus.

Despite the flurry of Leninist rhetoric emanating from Tito in the early 1970s, the practice as it evolved, in the 1970s, was only tenuously related to the Leninist model that had served Yugoslavia so well in the 1940s. In the 1980s, under pressure of events (most of which were inextricably linked to Yugoslavia's external environment), the Republic of Serbia, in a political process that was characteristically redistributive, set out systematically to reverse the Titoist trend toward virtual republic status for Kosovo. At the Federation level, in handling the most acute crisis provoked by Yugoslavia's international debt, the Federal Executive Council acted by the consensual policy process that exemplifies crisis politics the world around. Absent the manifest crisis and absent the consensus or the resources necessary for the pork barrel, distributional, politics as usual, the FEC, armed with Articles 301 and 302 of the 1974 Constitution, managed to govern.

The third "cut" (described in Chapters 4 and 5) at the impact of international-national linkages on the political evolution of Yugoslavia pertained to regime-society relations. In that realm as well, Yugoslav elite attitudes paralleled the Soviet perspective. In the early post-World War II years, the regime vigorously pursued measures designed to atomize and mobilize the citizenry; it set out systematically to insulate them from noncommunist influences and to extricate the regime from mass constraints. With regard to individual ties abroad, specifically, the introduction of communist rule implied a view that migration was virtually treasonous: the dictatorship of the proletariat signified not only that citizens would be precluded control over the political elite through an effective voice but denied the right of exit as well. In that sense, the iron curtain did extend from "Stettin in the Baltic to Trieste in the Adriatic."

Following Stalin's break with Tito and the gradual decompression throughout the 1950s, however, the idea that going abroad was treasonous began to be rethought. By the early 1960s, the Yugoslav leadership began to reverse its stance toward contacts between the Yugoslav citizenry and the

138

outside world. With the economic reforms in 1965 and the ouster of Ran-kovic in 1966, a public policy choice in favor of opening the borders had been made. The result was an enormous increase in the movement of persons across Yugoslav borders. Tourism in Yugoslavia burgeoned. More importantly, the outflow of Yugoslavs increased dramatically. In the changed political context, some 40,000 Yugoslavs crossed the border in 1970 daily, whereas roughly 500 daily had crossed the border in 1960. By the early 1970s, a million or more Yugoslav workers and their families had gone abroad to earn a living in capitalist Western Europe, North America, and Australia. With respect to its borders and the links of its citizenry to the international labor market, the conscious choice of Yugoslav communist elites had rendered Yugoslavia more like Greece and Turkey than Bulgaria and Romania.

Given such a political decision, the search for an explanation as to who migrates took us in two directions. The first direction was that of perception and the capacity to empathize, in Daniel Lerner's sense, that is, to envisage oneself in another context, a capacity that is linked with the passing of traditional society. We saw in Chapter 4 that the most insular and least modern regions, Kosovo and Montenegro, were least represented in the migration flows. Such a finding is consistent with the notion that at certain low levels of modernization, citizens from regions of a national state may be sufficiently nonmobilized as to be unaware of opportunities outside their village, much less outside the country. Given such knowledge, and the political decision to open the borders, the Yugoslav migration pattern has been driven largely by economic considerations. The result has been that the trend with respect to migration for the various republics and autonomous regions has been relatively easy to specify. Slovenia has evolved from a major exporter of migrant workers in the mid-1960s to a republic that in the mid-1980s sends few of its workers abroad and instead is a net importer of *gastarbeiter*, as it were, from other republics of Yugoslavia. Likewise, major changes took place with respect to Croatia in the 1970s, and bid fair to continue throughout the 1980s. In 1970 Croatia accounted for a disproportionately large share of the Yugoslav workers abroad. So many people from Croatia and ethnic Croatians were abroad at the beginning of the 1970s as to constitute a central focus of the discontent that fueled the resurgence of Croatian nationalism in the early 1970s. Ironically, the most vociferous complaints occurred just at a time when "objective factors" began to mitigate the impetus to migrate. By the 1970s, however, Croatia had modernized substantially in comparison with its situation in 1965 and the onset of the economic reform. By the 1981 census, the external migration was no longer a preponderantly Croatian phenomenon, and the distinctive role of Croatia in the Yugoslav external migration was a thing of the past.

139

The trend seems to be that in the late 1980s the seventh republic is likely to be an increasingly Serbian rather than a Croatian phenomenon. In the 1981 census the number of persons abroad from Serbia proper slightly exceeded the number from Croatia, and given the substantial unemployment in Serbia, it is easy to imagine a revived European economy having a considerable draw for persons from Serbia in the late 1980s. Likewise, in absolute numbers, Bosnia-Hercegovina and especially Macedonia should continue to be major exporters of migrant workers, presuming the availability of jobs in Western Europe. In percentage terms, however, the largest increments are likely to come from Montenegro and Kosovo. For the remainder of the 1980s, consequently, the phalanx of problems that attend the outmigration of workers will not burden the northern republics of Slovenia and Croatia to a great degree. Slovenia, especially, is much more likely to confront problems attending the immigration of guest workers from lesser developed Yugoslav republics. For Yugoslavia as a whole, however, it had become apparent by the beginning of the 1970s that the seventh republic of workers and their families abroad was not a temporary phenomenon, but rather a basically fixed feature of the Yugoslav political system.

As such, Yugoslav elites have had to address the issue of how to go about "governing" the citizens of that seventh republic—to control, to inform, to socialize, etc.—while they were abroad. And, indeed, during the 1970s and 1980s the patterns political scientists associate with governing are found in the relations between the Yugoslav leadership and Yugoslav citizens abroad. Regime-mass relations in the six Yugoslav republics find some counterpart in the way Yugoslav authorities deal with the Yugoslav workers abroad. The latter are punished for acts committed abroad that are illegal in Yugoslavia; they are exposed to Yugoslav press, radio, and television; they are serviced by Yugoslav social workers; and they are taught about Yugoslavia by Yugoslav teachers.

In turn, the phenomenon of the seventh republic feeds back upon regime-society relations in Yugoslavia itself. More than anything else perhaps, the seventh republic has legitimated the sense that Yugoslavia is an open country. The decision to open the country to the outmigration of workers set in motion what are very likely irreversible trends. Simply put, regardless of elite values, the seventh republic constrains the regime's alternatives. The return to a society of closed boundaries is highly implausible, even should elites desire such an option. The leadership needs Yugoslav workers abroad and needs their remittances—which now amount to billions of U. S. dollars annually. Actions that would severely reduce the amount of those remittances are exceedingly unlikely. Likewise, the open borders policy ties Yugoslav mass culture inextricably to European mass culture in ways that render the costs of achieving a monopoly over the socialization process prohibitive.

140

In brief, a policy of openness, while probably increasing citizen loyalty, alters the distribution of power between regime and society in ways that effectively preclude a strategy of mass mobilization. It is not just voice but exit in Hirschman's terms that allows society to limit the behavior of elites.

SEVERAL broader implications flowed from this study. For the study of Yugoslavia per se, perhaps three important conclusions stand out. First, if we can extrapolate trends in the past at all to current and future developments, then it follows that any attempt to assess the future political evolution of Yugoslavia without placing Yugoslavia in the context of its international environment will be ill-founded. Although this is a theme that has permeated this book, it nevertheless bears italicizing. There is much to be gained in understanding Yugoslav politics in the 1980s by examining, for instance, the national question again; by studying in greater depth the evolving changes of key Yugoslav political concepts such as democratic centralism or self management; or by systematically assessing intra-Yugoslav regional development issues. Nevertheless, readers should by now realize that such putatively domestic forces for change as nationalism, or ostensibly domestic problems as regional development or allegedly home-grown political concepts as self-management turn out to be incomprehensible in the Yugoslav setting absent an attention to international-national linkages. It is not just that ostensibly domestic phenomena have on inspection a manifestly transnational flavor. One cannot write the history of the internal evolution of post-World War II Yugoslavia without describing the role of actors outside Yugoslavia, whether those actors be international organizations (the IMF and the European Common Market most notably); states (e.g., the Soviet Union, the United States, the FRG, Albania); the Yugoslav political emigration, or the Yugoslav *gastarbeiter* in Western Europe.

This study draws on events extending through 1983; one could draw the chronological line anywhere and the centrality of the international-national links to an understanding of Yugoslav political evolution would remain. Consider, for instance, the eighteen months extending through calendar 1984 and the first half of 1985. Only a fully researched and very careful study would elaborate the exact role of the IMF in the playing out in 1984-1985 of the long-running story of Yugoslav indebtedness/balance of payment problems, the ongoing policy dialogue relating to the role of federal institutions, republic party organizations, and the market in resource allocation decisions. Has the IMF dictated internal changes to a reluctant Yugoslav federal government? Or, as I would anticipate, has the IMF made it politically easier for the federal government to do that which the FEC knows to be necessary while minimizing its political costs? Did, as has been speculated with some seriousness, Milka Planic, the Yugoslav prime minister, go home and thank God for the IMF? (A. Ross Johnson, private communication.) How, similarly, to assess the evolving relations between Albanians and Serbs within SR Serbia without detailing the effects of the leadership succession in Albania or understand the treatment of intellectuals in 1984-1985 without assessing the role of external actors including Amnesty International, European and American lawyers and public figures, and perhaps others such as the United States government as well? Indeed, the role of external actors in Yugoslav internal politics may, if anything, intensify in the near term. Yugoslavia's inflation and balance of payments problem will not soon dissipate and indeed will likely become exacerbated in the short term as the country adjusts to decisions to increase the role of the market in establishing prices. Furthermore, there is considerable likelihood that issues relative to the Yugoslav internal migration, Yugoslav external migration, and Serbian nationalism will be conjoined politically.

Second, the role of conscious policy choices in mediating the impact of changes or inputs from the external environment needs to be stressed. The link of the political evolution of Yugoslavia to the external environment is not a mechanistic one. We saw that nonalignment led to self-management, but it need not have done so. Analogously, conscious decisions had to be made to open the borders and political careers had to be ended in order to implement the 1965 economic reform, a decision that fundamentally tied Yugoslav market socialism to the international market. By the same token, political careers have been ended ostensibly to prevent the country from leaning too far in an Eastern (Aleksandar Rankovic) or a Western direction (Djilas, Stane Kavcic). Again, concrete decisions were taken to attempt to "govern" the workers abroad, regardless of whether governing implies the exercise of legal sanctions against Yugoslavs for acts committed abroad or the provision of social services to Yugoslav *gastarbeiter* in the German Federal Republic. Beyond the role of conscious acts in the determination of particular events, moreover, there is the prevalent issue of the general orientation of Yugoslav elites to the opportunities and challenges posed by close links to the international system. The costs of interdependence were brought home forcefully by the stagnation in Europe after the 1973 energy shock and by Yugoslavia's foreign indebtedness in the 1980s. Time and again, however, Yugoslav elites have rejected the counsel of those within Yugoslavia and abroad who champion self-reliance in the sense of insulation from the international system. Instead, over the years, Yugoslav elites have repeatedly demonstrated that the careful cultivation of plural external sources can strengthen their ability to govern. They have acted, and I suspect continue to act, as though they believe they can reduce the political costs of controversial acts by alleging that the steps taken were in response to external pressures. Certainly, they have been highly effective in extracting resources from the international system by playing West and East against each other.

A third main point flows directly from the second: elite decisions to open the country have set in motion processes that severely constrain the likely future evolution of the Yugoslav political institutions. After forty years of communist rule, Yugoslavia is still a one-party system and the political rhetoric is still replete with references to phrases that are traditional in the Marxist-Leninist repertoire. Moreover, the verbiage is not mere rhetoric; there is a mobilization of bias against certain policy options that can only be understood by reference to the doctrinal utterances of the eminently pragmatic elites governing Yugoslavia in the 1980s. These facts nothwithstanding, the opening of the borders to the flow of people and the opening of the economy to the effects of the international market greatly reduced the domain of politics and the political system. Moreover, the regime's adoption of a policy of openness to the international system has turned out to have long-term consequences for the political system: authoritarian rule and exit in Hirschman's sense seem perfectly compatible in Yugoslavia and elsewhere, but the Yugoslav case suggests that exit and a thoroughgoing mobilization strategy are incompatible. A policy of openness alters the distribution of power between regime and society in ways that effectively preclude a strategy of mass mobilization. Exit precludes, in Hirschman's words, "totalitarian expansionist tyrannies" [1970, p. 59]. At the same time, by creating an escape valve, the opening of the borders in Yugoslavia probably also increased citizen loyalty and decreased the likelihood of the mobilization of counter-elites bent on transforming the political system in a thoroughly pluralist fashion. Just as exit precludes Yugoslav totalitarianism, it may facilitate Yugoslav authoritarianism in much the way that Hirschman reports that "exit-competition" enhances the durability of an organization like the Nigerian Railway Corporation that is "unambitious and escapable" [p. 59; italics omitted].

This observation does not imply that to encourage the evolution of Yugoslavia in directions that allow for greater societal voice necessitates limiting exit. It does suggest very hard thinking about the choices that confront Yugoslav foreign policy and the evolution of the Yugoslav political system. The key at this juncture is to encourage market discipline. A major finding about Yugoslav political institutions that emerges from this study is that Yugoslav political leaders have struggled assiduously to create a political system that purposefully eschews economically rational decisions involving the careful weighing of opportunity costs when politically consensual decisions based on formulas that cut in all the relevant actors are possible. When hard choices have had to be made, however, Burg (1983) and this study have shown that the 1974 Yugoslav Constitution has pro-

143

vided, thus far, the institutional wherewithal for effective governance in the absence of consensus.

To enhance the capacity to govern and to reduce somewhat the proclivity to cut in all the relevant players without regard to efficiency concerns probably requires some recentralization (or "refederalization" as the Yugoslavs euphemistically describe it). Given the conditions Yugoslav elites face in the 1980s, decisionmaking under taut conditions almost always carries with it a centralizing thrust. There is a temptation as well for actors outside a state who seek to encourage financial discipline to wish, or to be seen as wishing, to identify clear lines of command in the debtor state, in this instance, Yugoslavia. There is a real danger in such conditions that the external actors—who can play a major role in reducing the political costs for central decisionmakers in taking hard decisions—will be seen as siding with one or more ethnic groups. With respect to Yugoslavia, this danger is especially likely against the backdrop of the resurgence of Serbian nationalism and the visceral—rightly or wrongly—equation by Slovenes, Croats, and Kosovars of centralization with Serbian hegemonism.

If what one is striving for is a Yugoslavia in which citizen voice is a more effective influence on governmental policies, the discipline which Yugoslavia requires at this juncture is that which flows from devolving power from the political system to the market, not the recentralization of power to the Federation at the expense of the republics. It pays to remember that consensus is an essential *sine qua non* of democratization. There is, to be sure, an ironic and unavoidable paradox here: it may sometimes be necessary to strengthen central political institutions, the National Bank for example, at the expense of republic institutions *in order to increase* the scope of the market. (Increasing the scope of the market would have the desirable effect of reducing the domain of the republic party organizations.) In like fashion, those strands in Yugoslav thinking that see Yugoslavia's future as being tied to close relations with Western multinationals should be encouraged. (The most prominent such voice was Vladimir Bakaric.) In this regard, consequently, the decision Yugoslav elites took in the years between 1982 and 1984 to intensify Yugoslavia's ties to the international market warrants encouragement. The economic reasons why this is so are obvious: such a commitment will make for more rational prices, will reduce the amount of institutionalized inflation, and increase the fiscal responsibility of enterprises and banks. The point here is a political one. Such ties will go a long way toward effecting the future political evolution of Yugoslavia in directions that increase the ability of the citizenry to influence policy outcomes and resource allocation decisions.

THESE points about the relation of Yugoslav political evolution to Yugoslavia's external evolution suggest the pertinence of this study to the broader area of comparative and international politics as well. Certain generalizations follow if the Yugoslav experience is relevant to that of other states or classes of states. For one thing, the impact of international-national linkages on the political evolution of Yugoslavia should sensitize us to the potential relevance of such linkages elsewhere as well. This is not a trivial point: I would wager that a very sizable fraction of comparative politics specialists, if asked to explain why multiparty democracy is the characteristic form of government in Western Europe, would focus on historical experiences, modernization, and political culture. Yet the principal explanation for the political systems of the contemporary states of Europe is the position of the American, British, and Soviet armies at the end of World War II. In the Yugoslav setting the change in the international environment created a context conducive to far-reaching changes in foreign policy, political institutions, and regime-society relations. This suggests that those who would extrapolate from either the Soviet model or the satellite model may have an overly narrow and deterministic view of the prospective political evolution of states headed by elites professing to be Marxist-Leninists. Judging by the Yugoslav experience, it is one thing to predict the political evolution of such states if they operate within the Soviet political-military ambit (and even there the cumulative effects of incremental changes may be quite substantial) and quite another to anticipate how an analogous state will evolve its institutions, its foreign policy, or its relations with its citizenry absent a major Soviet presence.

Likewise, I cannot stress overmuch the implication that the Yugoslav case bears out the assertion first advanced out of Hirschman's study of monopolies: to wit, that totalitarianism entails the closing of the state's borders. Beyond that, an authoritarian regime that permits exit is giving up by so doing the capacity to mobilize its citizenry—to nationalize affect in Alex Inkeles' words—in the manner of a totalitarian regime. (In so doing, it may be enhancing its stability but that is another issue.)

A second consideration of general significance to the study of comparative and international politics involves our thinking about the external penetration of political systems. The findings of this study reinforce the tendency in the world politics literature to argue that external penetration per se is not necessarily damaging to, and may indeed enhance, a state's capacity to govern [Huntington, 1973]. Dependency theorists and students of Soviet penetration of Eastern Europe alike have contributed to the widespread failure to recognize this possibility by not differentiating between penetration and single-source penetration. Not only does Yugoslavia illustrate the blessings of occupying a saddle-point position in a loosely bipolar world. Additionally, it represents evidence that plural penetration can increase a state's freedom to maneuver internationally and also allow its elites to maximize the resources available with which to pursue its internal development strat-

145

egy. Moreover, note must be taken of the direction of external penetration. Heretofore, virtually all studies of political penetration of one state by another have assumed that it involves a greater power intruding itself in the policy process of a lesser state. Yugoslavia's pattern of governing the million Yugoslav workers and their families abroad represents an instance of the penetration of more powerful and developed states by a lesser one. As daily accounts of terrorist activity in Europe bear painful witness, Yugoslavia is not alone in such behavior, though how prevalent such occurrences are is beyond the range of this study. In any event, the phenomenon of small-state penetration of larger states is one that requires some fundamental adjustments in basic paradigms in international and comparative politics.

This in turn leads to a general comment about the academic study of comparative and international politics. A study of international-national linkages and the political evolution of Yugoslavia underlines the extent to which communist studies have lost the attributes of normal science as a result of the growing irrelevance of the Soviet and satellite models which had served as the paradigms for communist studies.

My belief is that in like fashion this study underlines the need for a paradigm shift in the study of international and comparative politics. Exactly what shape a new paradigm will take is not something that derives from this study. A notion that is reinforced by this book—and which is contrary to conventional wisdom in comparative politics—is that conceiving of policy processes, the content of which is in considerable measure driven by the nature of issue area, is appropriate for authoritarian as well as pluralist systems. With respect specifically to the central theme of international-national linkages, what I trust emerges from this study is the artificiality of thinking of international politics as politics between states and other international actors, and comparative politics as politics within a state. To the extent Yugoslavia is typical of many contemporary states, it is far more appropriate to think of comparative politics as focusing on the evolution and performance of political systems and international politics as involving efforts by international actors to influence the behavior of other states and international actors. Thinking of comparative and international politics in this way will lead inevitably to some convergence in the two areas of inquiry. That is as it should be: an understanding of both comparative and international politics will be enhanced in the process. The study of international-influence attempts—international politics—is enhanced if we focus not only on direct efforts as has been the traditional focus of international politics, but if we extend the analysis to examine the role of indirect influence attempts through the participation of states, international organizations, and groups outside a nation state's borders in the political processes and institutions of another state. Our understanding of the evolution and performance of political systems—comparative politics—likewise is enhanced when we extend, as has been done in analyzing the political evolution of Yugoslavia, our horizons beyond the confines of the territorial boundaries of the state. In so doing, we will find instances when the state's capacity to govern is enhanced by encouraging the penetration of the political system by plural international actors. We will also find that the domain of a state, even a small state, is not coterminous with its territorial confines. We will find that a full appreciation of the extractive capability of states can be achieved only by assessing the resources available in the external environment in addition to those in the domestic environment. The study of international-national linkages as they relate to Yugoslavia drives home the proposition that more accurate answers to questions about the evolution and performance of political systems and institutions are achieved by assessing in quite concrete terms the difference it makes for a state's political evolution that that state exists in an international environment as well as a domestic one.

SELECTED BIBLIOGRAPHY

Adamic, Louis. 1952. *The Eagle and the Roots.* Garden City, N. Y.: Doubleday and Company.

Almond, Gabriel A. 1960. "A Functional Approach to Comparative Politics," in Almond and James S. Coleman, eds., *The Politics of Developing Areas.* Princeton: Princeton University Press.

Bakaric, Vladimir. 1967. *Aktuelni problemi sadasnje etape revolucije.* Zagreb: Stvarnost.

Baletic, Zvonimir. 1965. "Medjunarodne migracije i nase savremene migracije." *Nase teme,* No. 5, 680-700.

Baskin, Mark. 1983. "Crisis in Kosovo." *Problems of Communism* (March-April 1983), 61-74.

Bass, Robert, and Elizabeth Marbury, eds. 1957. *The Soviet-Yugoslav Controversy, 1949-1958: A Documentary Record.* New York: Prospect Books.

Baucic, Ivo. 1970. *Porijeklo i struktura radnika iz Jugoslavije u SR Njemackoj.* Zagreb: Institut za geografiju.

———. 1973. *Radnici u inozemstvu prema popisu stanounistva Jugoslavije 1971.* Zagreb: Institut za geografiju.

———. 1975. *Social Aspects of External Migration of Workers and the Yugoslav Experience in the Social Protection of Migrants.* Zagreb: Center for Migration Studies.

———. 1976. "Socijalni aspekti vanjskih migracija i jugoslavenska iskustva u socijalnoj zastiti migranata." *Rasprave o migracijama,* No. 24.

———. 1978. "The Position of European Migrants in the Political Life of Their Homeland: The Yugoslav Case." Unpublished paper.

———. 1979. "Stanje vanjskih migracija iz Jugoslavije krajem sedamdesetih godina." *Rasprave o migracijama,* No. 57. Zagreb: Centar za istrazivanje migracija.

———. 1982. "Konacni rezultati popisa Jugoslavenskikh gradjana u inozemstvu." *Migracije,* Nos. 8-9, 319-334.

———, and Zivko Maravic. 1971. *Vracanje i zaposljavanje vanjskih migranata iz SR Hrvatske.* Zagreb: Institut za geografiju.

Bertsch, Gary K. 1971. "Nation Building in Yugoslavia: A Study of Political Integration and Additudinal Consensus." *Sage Professional Papers in Comparative Politics* 2, No. 01-022. Beverly Hills: Sage Publications.

Besker, Inoslav, ed. 1979. *Medjunarodni odnosi i vanjska politika socialisticke Jugoslavije: Studije i dokumenti.* Zagreb: Centar drustvenih djelatnosti Saveza socijalisticke omladine Hrvatske.

Bilandzic, Dusan. 1969. *Borba za samoupravni socijalizam u Jugoslaviji 1945-1969.* Zagreb: Institut za historiju radnickog pokreta Hrvatske.

———. 1981. "O osnovnim tendencijama drustvenog razvoja." *Nase teme,* No. 12, 1866.

149

Bornstein, Morris, Zvi Gitelman, and William Zimmerman, eds. 1981. *East-West Relations and the Future of Eastern Europe: Politics and Economics*. London: George Allen and Unwin.

Brzezinski, Zbigniew K. 1967. *The Soviet Bloc: Unity and Conflict*. Cambridge: Harvard University Press.

Burg, Steven L. 1983. *Conflict and Cohesion in Socialist Yugoslavia: Political Decision Making Since 1966*. Princeton: Princeton University Press.

Buric, Olivera. 1973. "Novi tip nepotpune pordice." *Sociologija* 15, No. 2, 268.

Cicin-Sain, Ante. 1983. "Promejena uloge deviznih doznaka i devizne stedneje," *Migracije*, No. 5, 165-173.

Committee to Aid Democratic Dissidents in Yugoslavia [CADDY]. 1983. *Bulletin*, Nos. 16, 19.

Dadic, Branko, ed. 1970. *Jugoslavija u svetu: Medjunarodni odnosi i spoljna politika Jugoslavije 1941-1969*. Beograd: Mladost.

Dean, Robert. "The Political Role of the Yugoslav Military." Unpublished paper, n.d.

Dedijer, Vladimir. 1953. *Tito Speaks: His Self-Portrait and Struggle with Stalin*. London: Weidenfeld and Nicolson.

Deutsch, Karl. 1966. "External Influences on the Internal Behavior of States," in R. Barry Farrell, ed., *Approaches to Comparative and International Politics*. Evanston, Ill.: Northwestern University Press.

Dimitrijevic, Vojin. 1982. *Disarmament and Security: Yugoslavia*. Geneva: United Nations Institute for Disarmament Research.

Djodan, Sime. 1969. "Regionalni ekonomski razvoj Jugoslavije." *Encyclopaedia moderna* 14, No. 10, 31-49.

Djurovic, Dragoljub, et al., eds. 1974. *The Constitution of the Socialist Federal Republic of Yugoslavia*. Belgrade: Secretariat of the Federal Assembly Information Service.

Easton, David. 1953. *The Political System: An Inquiry into the State of Political Science*. New York: Knopf.

Farkas, Richard P. 1975. *Yugoslav Economic Development and Political Change: The Relationship between Economic Managers and Policy-making Elites*. New York: Praeger.

Farrell, R. Barry. 1956. *Yugoslavia and the Soviet Union 1948-1956*. Hamden, Conn.: Shoe String Press.

Grecic, Vladimir. 1975. *Savremene migracije radne snage u Evropi*. Beograd: Institut za medjunarodnu politiku i privredu.

Gurr, Ted Robert. 1974. "Persistence and Change in Political Systems, 1800-1971." *American Political Science Review* 68, No. 4 (December), 1484-1504.

Hirschman, Albert O. 1970. *Exit, Voice, and Loyalty: Responses to Decline in Firms, Organizations, and States*. Cambridge: Harvard University Press.

———. 1978. "Exit, Voice, and the State." *World Politics* 31, No. 1, 90-108.

Hoover Institution. 1980. *Yearbook of International Communist Affairs*. Stanford.

Hovet, Thomas. 1960. *Bloc Politics in the U. N.* Cambridge: Harvard University Press.

Huntington, Samuel P. 1973. "Transnational Organizations in World Politics." *World Politics* 25, No. 3, 364-365.

Jacobson, Harold K., and William Zimmerman, eds. 1969. *The Shaping of Foreign Policy*. New York: Atherton Press.

Johnson, A. Ross. 1972. *The Transformation of Communist Ideology: The Yugoslav Case, 1945-1953*. Cambridge: The MIT Press.

————. 1978. *The Role of the Military in Communist Yugoslavia: An Historical Sketch*, Rand Paper P-6070. Santa Monica: The Rand Corporation.

Jones, Christopher D. 1981. *Soviet Influence in Eastern Europe: Political Autonomy and the Warsaw Pact*. New York: Praeger.

Kardelj, Edvard. 1978. *Pravci razvoja politickog sistema socijalistickog samou-pravljanja*. Beograd: *Komunist*.

Komarica, Zvonimir. 1970. *Jugoslavija u savremenim evropskim migracijama*. Zagreb: Ekonomski institut.

Kuhn, Thomas S. 1962. *The Structure of Scientific Revolutions*. Chicago: University of Chicago Press.

LaPalombara, Joseph. 1975. "Monoliths or Plural Systems: Through Conceptual Lenses Darkly." *Studies in Comparative Communism* 8, No. 3 (Autumn 1975), 305-332.

Lerner, Daniel. 1964. *The Passing of Traditional Society*. New York: Free Press.

Letic, Franjo. 1977. *Informiranje i informiranost vanjskih migranata iz SR Hrvatske o zbivanjima u domovini*. Zagreb: Centar za istrazivanje migracija.

Linden, Ronald H. "Responses to Interdependence: The Impact of International Change on Romania and Yugoslavia." Paper written for the National Council for Soviet and East European Research.

Linden, Ronald H. 1982. "The Security Bind in East Europe." *International Studies Quarterly* 26, No. 2, 155-189.

Lowi, Theodore J. 1964. "American Business, Public Policy, Case Studies and Political Theory." *World Politics* 16, No. 4, 677-715.

Lustick, Ian. 1979. "Stability in Deeply Divided Societies: Consociationalism versus Control." *World Politics* 31, No. 3, 325-344.

Markovic, Dragan, and Savo Krzavac. 1978. *Liberalizam od Djilasa do danas: Politicka kriza u Savez komunista Srbije i novi revolucionarni kurs*. Beograd: Sloboda.

Mates, Leo. 1972. *Nonalignment: Theory and Current Policy*. New York: Oceana.

Micovic, Vojislav. 1977. *Otvorenost Jugoslavije prema svetu*. Beograd: Sloboda.

Micunovic, Veljko. 1980. *Moscow Diary*. Garden City, N.Y.: Doubleday and Company.

Milojevic, Aleksa, and Vladimir Sultanovic. 1972. "Zaposljavanje u inostranstvu." *Pregled* 252, No. 1, 33-47.

Mladenovic, Mihailo. 1979. "Neka iskustva dosadasnoe politika brzeg razvoja privredno nedovoljno razvijenih republika i pokrajine Kosovo." *Gledista*, Nos. 11-12, 3-17

Mujacic, Mahmut. 1978. "Neke karakteristike procesa dogovaranja republika i autonomnih pokrajina." *Politicka misao* 4, 543-561.

Nejasmic, Ivica. 1981. "Povratak Jugoslavenskih vanjskih migranata i njihovo ukljucivanje u gospodarski i drustveni zivot zemlje." *Rasprave o migracijama*, No. 73.

OECD. 1975. (Organization for Economic Cooperation and Development). "Services for Returning Migrant Workers," *Joint Project*.

OECD. 1982. "Sistem stalnog pracenja migracija (SOPEMI) izvestaj za 1981 godinu." *Rasprave o migracijama*, No. 76.

Okun, T. 1973. "Inostrannye rabochie v Zapadnoi Germanii." *Mirovaia ekonomika i mezhdunarodnye otnosheniia*, No. 3, 137-138.

Petkovic, Ranko. 1983. "Untenability of the Assertions on the Crisis of the Policy and Movement of Non-Alignment." *Review of International Affairs* 34, No. 3 (March), 787, 789.

Polovina, Svetislav. 1969. "Migraciona kretanja u Evropi i njihovo ekonomsko-drustveno znacenje." *Nase teme*, No. 12, 1949-1950.

Ra'anan, Gavriel D. 1977. *Yugoslavia After Tito: Scenarios and Implications*. Boulder, Colo.: Westview Press.

Rosenau, James N. 1971. *The Scientific Study of Foreign Policy*. New York: Free Press.

Rosenau, James N., ed. 1967. *Domestic Sources of Policy*. New York: Free Press.

Rubinstein, Alvin Z. 1970. *Yugoslavia and the Non-Aligned World*. Princeton: Princeton University Press.

Rus, Veljko. 1972. "Current Relations among the Yugoslav Nationalities: Questions for Discussion." *International Journal of Politics* 2, No. 1, 13-14.

Rusinow, Dennison. 1977. *The Yugoslav Experiment 1968-1974*. London: C. Hurst and Company.

Shoup, Paul. 1968. *Communism and the Yugoslav National Question*. New York: Columbia University Press.

Silberman, Laurence. 1977. "Yugoslavia's 'Old' Communism: Europe's Fiddler on the roof." *Foreign Policy*, No. 26, 3-27.

Singleton, Fred. 1976. *Twentieth-Century Yugoslavia*. New York: Columbia University Press.

Stankovic, Slobodan, "Initial Yugoslav Reactions to Soviet Invasion of Yugoslavia." *Radio Free Europe Research*, January 4, 1980, 1-3.

Strbac, Cedomir. 1975. *Jugoslavija i odnosi izmedju socijalistickih zemalja: Sukob KPJ i Informbiroa*. Beograd: Institut za medjunarodnu politiku i privredu.

Suvar, Stipe. 1971. "Drustvena pokretljivost i razvojne perspektive jugoslovenskog drustva." *Gledista* 12, Nos. 11-12 (November-December), 1489-1567.

Tadic, Stipe. 1975. "Neki ekonomski ucinci vanjskih migracija iz Jugoslavije" *Rasprave o migracijama*, No. 15.

Tanic, Zivan. 1974. *Seljaci na evropskim raskrsnicama: Analiza ekonomskih migracija*. Beograd: Institut drustvenih nauka, Centar za socioloska istrazivanja.

Terry, Sarah M., ed. 1984. *Soviet Relations with Eastern Europe*. New Haven: Yale University Press.

Tito, Josip Broz. 1959. *Govori i clanci 1941-1957*, Vols. 1 and 2. Zagreb: Naprijed.

Tos, Nikola et al. 1978. *Slovenski radnici u FR Njemachkoj*. Ljubljana: Ljabljana.

Ulam, Adam B. 1952. *Titoism and the Cominform*. Cambridge: Harvard University Press.

U. S. Agency for International Development. 1961, 1973, 1978. *U. S. Foreign Assistance and Assistance for International Organizations*. Washington, D.C.: U.S. Government Printing Office.

U. S. Department of State. 1974. *Foreign Relations of the United States, 1948*, Vol. 4, *Eastern Europe-Soviet Union*. Washington, D. C.: U. S. Government Printing Office.

————. 1976. *Foreign Relations of the United States, 1949*, Vol. 5, *Eastern Europe-Soviet Union*. Washington, D. C.: U. S. Government Printing Office.

Vinski, Ivo. 1971. "Drustveni proizvod Jugoslavije i zemalja istoka i zapada" *Ekonomski pregled*, Nos. 10-11, 589-627.

Vinski, Ivo. 1972. "Kolektivna potrosnja u Jugoslaviji, 1970-1985." *Ekonomski pregled*, Nos. 11-12, 490-512.

Vucinich, Wayne S., ed. 1982. *At the Brink of War and Peace: The Tito-Stalin Split*. Volume 10 in *War and Society in East Central Europe*. New York: Social Science Monographs, Brooklyn College Press.

Wilson, Duncan. 1979. *Tito's Yugoslavia*. Cambridge: Cambridge University Press.

Wolfers, Arnold. 1962. *Discord and Collaboration: Essays on International Politics*. Baltimore: Johns Hopkins Press, 1962.

Yugoslav Ministry of Foreign Affairs. 1951. *White Book on Aggressive Activities by the Governments of the USSR, Poland, Czechoslovakia, Hungary, Romania, Bulgaria, and Albania Towards Yugoslavia*. Belgrade.

Zimmerman, William. 1973. "Issue Area and Foreign-Policy Process: A Research Note in Search of a General Theory." *American Political Science Review* 67, No. 4 (December), 1204-1212.

————. 1976. "The Tito Succession and the Evolution of Yugoslav Politics." *Studies in Comparative Communism* 9, Nos. 1 and 2 (Spring-Summer), 62-79.

Zupanov, Josip. 1981. "Aktualni drustveni trenutak." *Nase teme* 25, No. 12, 1945-1955.

Relevant Yugoslav periodicals and Western translations of Yugoslav materials

Borba
Danas
Ekonomska politika
Ekonomski pregled
Encyclopaedia moderna
Foreign Broadcast Information
  Service, Daily Report: Eastern
  Europe [*FBIS*]
Gledista
Indeks
Joint Translation Service
Komunist
NIN (Nedeljne informativne novine)

Nase teme
Politicka misao
Politika
Pregled
Radio Free Europe Research
  [RFE *Research*]
Rasprave o migracijama
Review of International Affairs
Sluzbeni list
Sociologija
Statisticki godisnjak Jugoslavije
Studentski list
Vjesnik

INDEX

Yugoslavia (*cont.*)
  succession issue, 11, 39, 40, 46, 48
  trade relations, 13, 19, 20, 32-33, 36, 41,
    42, 133, 134-135
  trade unions, 44, 45, 46, 47, 126
  unemployment, 4, 5
  United Nations and, 14, 26, 30-32, 59-61
  Western European links, 9, 15-16, 20, 23,
    25, 26, 32, 36, 41, 44, 74-75, 78-81,
    87, 92-93, 96, 99, 103, 109, 110, 112,
    123-24, 133, 139, 140, 141, 142
  women in the workforce, 87, 100

  workers' self-management, *see* Yugo-
    slavia, self-management
  Yugoslav-Soviet relations, 5, 9, 16, 17, 18,
    19, 20, 23-24, 26, 42, 94, 132, 133;
    Yugoslav-Soviet rapprochement, 14
  Yugoslav-U.S. relations, 15, 23, 58, 95

Zagreb, 10, 46, 47, 88, 111, 120, 136
Zagreb University, 4, 57, 58, 73
Zanko, Milos, 10
Zimmerman, William, 29, 48

Library of Congress Cataloging-in-Publication Data

Zimmerman, William, 1936-
Open borders, nonalignment, and the political
evolution of Yugoslavia.

Bibliography: p.
Includes index.
1. Yugoslavia—Politics and government—1945-   .
2. Yugoslavia—Emigration and immigration—Government policy.
3. Yugoslavia—Nonalignment.   I. Title.

JN9662.Z56 1987   949.7'02   86-25145
ISBN 0-691-07730-4 (alk. paper)

William Zimmerman is Professor of Political Science at the
University of Michigan and is the author of *Soviet Perspectives
on International Relations, 1957-1967* (Princeton).